# HOW TO
# WRITE LIKE
# CHEKHOV

ANTON CHEKHOV was born in 1860 in Taganrog, a port on the Sea of Azov. His father, a shopkeeper, was the son of a peasant who bought himself and his family out of serfdom. Chekhov began to write short stories while studying at the University of Moscow, and after graduating from medical school he embraced both professions: medicine as his "lawful wife" and literature as his "mistress." While continuing to write short stories, Chekhov became interested in the theater and, early in his career, began to write plays. His first successful full-length play, *The Sea Gull*, was produced in 1896, followed by *Uncle Vanya* and *The Three Sisters*. *The Cherry Orchard* appeared in 1904, and in the same year Chekhov, who had long suffered from tuberculosis, died at the age of forty-four.

Co-editor PIERO BRUNELLO is a professor of social history at the University of Venice in Italy.

Co-editor and translator LENA LENČEK is professor of Russian and the humanities at Reed College in Portland, Oregon, and the author, editor, co-author, and co-editor of more than a dozen books, including *Beach: Stories by the Sand and Sea*. She has recently annotated a new edition of Tolstoy's *War and Peace*. She lives in Portland, Oregon.

*Anton Chekhov*

# HOW TO
# WRITE LIKE
# CHEKHOV

## ADVICE AND INSPIRATION,
## STRAIGHT FROM HIS OWN LETTERS
## AND WORK

---

*Edited and introduced by*
## Piero Brunello and Lena Lenček

*Translated from the Russian and Italian by*
## Lena Lenček

Da Capo
∞
LIFE
LONG

A MEMBER OF THE PERSEUS BOOKS GROUP

Part One © 2002 by Minimum Fax
Part Two © 2004 by Piero Brunello and Minimum Fax
Translation © 2008 by Perseus Books Group

DESIGNED BY JEFF WILLIAMS
Set in 11.75-point Adobe Garamond by the Perseus Books Group

Cataloging-in-Publication data for this book is available from the Library of Congress.

First Da Capo Press edition 2008
This book is derived from two books previously published in Italy by Minimum Fax: *Senza trame e senza finale: 99 consigli di scrittura*, © 2002 by Minimum Fax, and *Scarpe buone e un quaderno di appunti: Come fare un reportage*, © 2004 by Piero Brunello and Minimum Fax. This edition is published by arrangement with Minimum Fax.

Chekhov, Anton Pavlovich, 1860-1904.
[Selections. English. 2008]
How to write like Chekhov : advice and inspiration, straight from his own letters and work / edited and introduced by Piero Brunello and Lena Lenček ; translated from the Russian and Italian by Lena Lenček. — 1st Da Capo Press ed.
        p. cm.
Includes bibliographical references.
ISBN 978-1-56924-259-9 (alk. paper)
1. Chekhov, Anton Pavlovich, 1860-1904--Translations into English. 2. Authorship. 3. Creation (Literary, artistic, etc.) I. Brunello, Piero, 1948- II. Lenček, Lena. III. Title.
PG3456.A13B78 2008
808'.02—dc22

                                                                2008024843

Published by Da Capo Press
A Member of the Perseus Books Group
www.dacapopress.com

Da Capo Press books are available at special discounts for bulk purchases in the United States by corporations, institutions, and other organizations. For more information, please contact the Special Markets Department at the Perseus Books Group, 2300 Chestnut Street, Suite 200, Philadelphia, PA 19103, or call (800) 810-4145, extension 5000, or e-mail special.markets@perseusbooks.com.

10 9 8 7 6 5 4 3 2 1

*To my father, Rado L. Lenček and my sister Bibi*
—L. L.

"In writing, it is not the head but
the seat that gets the job done."

RADO L. LENČEK (1921–2005)

# CONTENTS

## 2. SPECIFIC QUESTIONS

## PART TWO: DEMONSTRATION
### *Good Shoes and a Notebook*
— *55* —

### 3. THE PROJECT

## 4. THE REPORT

## 5. THE ACTUAL WRITING

# PREFACE

ঌৡৣৡৣৡ৸

THIS BOOK BEGAN LIFE AS TWO SEPARATE ITALIAN VOL-
umes, *No Plot, No Ending* and *Good Shoes and a Notebook*.[1] This English-language edition combines this material
between one set of covers, which makes sense for two reasons: it gives the reader direct access to Anton Chekhov's
nuggets of writing wisdom in the form of advice to writers
tucked in his correspondence, and it provides examples of
this advice in practice, in the form of excerpts from his nonfiction travel memoir *The Island of Sakhalin*.[2]

The notes that periodically amplify the primary text are by
Piero Brunello [P.B.] and myself [L.L.], and in part 2, "Good
Shoes and a Notebook," a dozen or so are by Chekhov himself
[A.C.]; those notes attributed to him here originally appeared
as notes to *The Island of Sakhalin*.

—LENA LENČEK

# INTRODUCTION
## BY PIERO BRUNELLO

❧

THIS VOLUME PRESENTS ANTON CHEKHOV'S ADVICE ON how to write. Its purpose is to transmit Chekhov's guidelines on becoming a good writer, and it is presented with the hope that these guidelines will be useful, in various ways, to novices and to experienced professional writers alike. Chekhov's detailed suggestions draw heavily on his own experience, both as a writer of short stories, plays, novellas, and nonfiction and as a discerning reader of literary texts. He knew the burden of solitude that comes with writing, the compulsive need to write, and the dispiriting sting of an indifferent reception.

*How to Write Like Chekhov* began as a collection of advice that over a period of time I excerpted from Chekhov's work to help with my own writing. One day it occurred to me that what this great writer had to say on the subject could be useful to others as well. I remembered, for instance, that Raymond Carver—who in addition to writing short stories and poems taught creative writing for many years—used to credit Chekhov with having had an "enormous influence" on his own work and that he too had echoed Chekhov's lessons: to stick to "plain but precise language"; to reject "words weighed down with uncontrolled emotion"; to deliver "serious testimony about our lives"; and to remember that critics "can alleviate the sense of solitude" experienced by those who write.[3] Thus was born the idea for a book, and one organized around several topics.

Part 1, "No Plot, No Ending," is almost exclusively composed of material taken from Chekhov's extensive correspondence between the years 1886 and 1902, much of it with editors, writers, family, and friends bitten by the writing bug. Famous for being generous with his time and his energy, Chekhov was besieged with manuscripts and requests for feedback. Excerpts from his replies are included here and organized into rubrics cued by the sorts of questions that plague all writers: general questions about the motives for writing, audience, topics, approach, timing, and scope; and specific topics such as truth, descriptions, characters, emotions, what to avoid, and how to deal with one's fellow writers.

After the theory of part 1, part 2, "Good Shoes and a Notebook," takes a different approach: concrete demonstrations taken largely from Chekhov's nonfiction travel memoir *The Island of Sakhalin.* Initially conceived as his doctoral dissertation in medicine, though never put to that use, this extraordinary exposé by Chekhov of the czarist penal system was undertaken in the scientific spirit of Claude Bernard, the nineteenth-century physiologist who championed philosophical skepticism as the fundamental tool of the medical researcher. "Experimenters must doubt," Barnard wrote in his groundbreaking *An Introduction to the Study of Experi-*

*mental Medicine*, "avoid fixed ideas, and always keep their freedom of mind."[4] Writers must do the same.

In *The Island of Sakhalin*, Chekhov makes few explicit statements on methodology; rather, he limits himself to the rare aside questioning the validity, for instance, of statistics, or official reports. By and large, he trusts what he is told. He interpolates into his travel notes, character sketches, and descriptions of the landscape concrete information, including demographic data, meteorological tables, and medical and crime statistics. Chekhov also says next to nothing about writing. Although, as his narrative unfolds, one senses Chekhov's finely tuned mind sifting, weighing, and measuring hearsay against firsthand knowledge, he keeps silent about matters touching on his art. This silence presented a challenge to me, as I specifically wished to mine explicit lessons from the text. In order to do this, I have sought, first, to understand what Chekhov was doing in the course of his journey, and second, to present the episodes and anecdotes he recounts as advice, both theoretical and practical.

I have decided to arrange this advice in a way that illustrates every stage involved in creating a nonfiction manuscript. I begin with the conception of the idea and the initial tasks of reading up on the topic, framing the questions, and entertaining doubts. Next, I pass on to the fieldwork, with its research strategies and maneuvers for collecting data. Finally, I turn to the production of the manuscript itself: the organization of the notes and documents, the actual process of writing, and the delivery of the completed text into the world. I have divided this process into three sections: "The Project,"

"The Report," and "The Actual Writing." Under each rubric, I identify a number of critical steps with a title and supply a brief explanation of the principle or "lesson" that is exemplified in the passage from Chekhov's text. The idea here is to give readers a concrete example of how the advice was implemented, on the assumption that having a model before one's eyes is the best route to mastering techniques.

The *Sakhalin* material is especially addressed to writers who, like Chekhov, are interested in discovering, exploring, and understanding the unknown. The modus operandi of his voyage of discovery is useful not only to writers who make long journeys and wish to write about them but also to those who want to understand life closer to home. Chekhov's prose is a model for writers who care less for plot than for "what transpires in the space of a breath, in the meeting of two glances, in the moment of suspense when everything is both obvious and arcane." Those are the words of the Italian journalist Francesca Sanvitale, speaking with reference to the work of Katherine Mansfield, a writer who shared Chekhov's view of "the external certainty of the world, the ferment in the continual flux of life," and believed that "the beauty of life is to be found in its kaleidoscopic appearance."[5] Mansfield, like many modern writers, admired Chekhov's peculiarly detached curiosity: "The artist watches life closely," she wrote in a letter in 1921. "He says softly, 'So this is life, huh?' And he sits down to try to express it."[6]

For Chekhov, there could be no contradiction between action and observation because for him observation—objective, scrupulous, open-minded, and profoundly respectful—was itself the most hopeful and productive form of action. Contemporary writers—for instance, the Italian Natalia Ginzburg (1916–91), recognize this fine balance between the "engagement" of the socially committed intellectual and the "disengagement" of the observer as "absolutely necessary, indispensable for a novelist."[7]

I have heard it said that dancers learn, not by watching the teacher or the star pupil, but by imitating those who are just a bit better than they are. The same holds for writing. I do not know how this works; I only know that one learns from Chekhov. Maybe, as Vladimir Nabokov suggested, this is due to his "phenomenal sociability"—"his constant readiness to hobnob with anyone at all, to sing with singers and to get drunk with drunkards."[8] This gregarious spirit emerges even in the collage of fragments taken from the research and writing program that Chekhov used in investigating a penal colony located on a remote island in the Sea of Okhotsk. And it is in this spirit of convivial collegiality that we offer this book. We hope that it will prove to be a useful guide and that it might even relieve the solitude of those who wish to write, who love to travel responsibly, and who keep close to their hearts the ideal of a kind of writing that is precise, honest, and engaged.

# INTRODUCTION
# BY LENA LENČEK

⚜

"A man needs only seven feet of earth."
"No, it's a corpse that needs seven feet, not a
man. A man needs the whole world."
—ANTON CHEKHOV[9]


AMONG NINETEENTH-CENTURY RUSSIAN AUTHORS, ANTON
Chekhov holds the record for worst publicists. Writers,
critics, and friends who in life professed boundless admiration for his work damned him with the kind of praise that
kills reputations. Here are some examples: "Tchekhov was
the poet of hopelessness. Stubbornly, sadly, monotonously,
during all the years of his literary activity, nearly a quarter of
a century long, Tchekhov was doing one thing alone: by one
means or another he was killing human hopes."[10] Or another, by his theatrical collaborator Constantin Stanislavsky:
"The Chekhov mood is that cave in which are kept all the
unseen and hardly palpable treasures of Chekhov's soul."[11]
Maxim Gorky, who owed Chekhov a vast debt of gratitude
for tireless mentoring and encouragement, came up with the
following: "The author's mind...shows up in hard outline

the monotonous roads, the crooked streets, the little squalid houses in which tiny, miserable people are stifled by boredom and laziness and fill the houses with an unintelligible, drowsy bustle."[12] Prerevolutionary and Soviet critics doggedly promoted Chekhov as a kind of aesthetic phenobarbital, labeling him as "a singer of twilight moods," "a poet of superfluous people," "a sick talent," "a poet of anguish," a voice of "world sorrow," and—the clincher in the bunch—an "optimopessimist."[13]

That after such an introduction—much of it crammed onto the back cover of a repulsive puce-and-avocado-colored paperback—I would have ventured into the gloom-shrouded isle of Chekhov still amazes me. I was eighteen and had made my way through an archipelago of Russian writers, from Pushkin through Tolstoy, and so far each stop had been a luminous revelation. I loved the way these wordsmiths and plot-meisters seized my imagination, drilled into the core of adolescent angst, and delivered answers to my deepest questions about why the world was the way it was. From Pushkin's effervescent irony, I passed to Gogol's sublime buffoonery to Turgenev's elegiac polemics, Dostoevsky's sin-your-way-to-Jesus verities, and the steely morality of Tolstoy clad in the velvet glove of flawless realism.

By the time I reached Chekhov, I was in full novel gear. I could cruise effortlessly through digression-studded, intricate plots, protracted philosophical ruminations, oddly gripping debates on obscure topics, and, of course, the rich roll call of characters identified by baroque naming protocols—

given name, patronymic, surname, plus a dozen affectionate and abusive derivatives. I was not prepared for brevity, nuance, and plotlessness.

Chekhov turned out to be a giant among writers: lapidary, subtle, generous, infectious, and respectful of his readers in ways that the other Russians with better PR could not even imagine. He published 568 stories in a lifetime that spanned a total of 44 years. He corresponded with all the major and minor writers, critics, and artists of his time; mentored dozens of aspiring authors; and left a legacy that included copious advice on the art of writing—and living—well.

# ICONOCLAST

Chekhov's contemporaries might have found him the incarnation of melancholy, but I rather suspect that they were at a loss for how to peg his startlingly novel voice. That elusive hovering between tragedy and comedy that marks his work is in fact the first murmuring of a characteristically modern consciousness and sensibility. By this I mean our unease with a spectrum of reductive explanations (ideologies, dogmas, organized religion), our skepticism, anxiety, appetite for every pleasure of the flesh, irony, and commitment to a single, terrifying value: freedom. Rich with the sociological, economic, and political complexities of late czarist Russia from which they draw their local color, Chekhov's stories offer few consolations to readers seeking escape from quotidian banalities or rules of conduct. They offer no palliatives, no ultimate solutions rooted in metaphysics.

Working at a time when Russian readers expected their writers to preach in the tones of Old Testament prophets, Chekhov was a bewildering anomaly. Since Peter the Great had revolutionized Russia "from above" by imposing a west European "high culture" and a stringently autocratic rule buttressed by Orthodoxy, secret police, and censorship, Russians had come to rely on their imaginative literature to perform the role that public discourse plays in the West. To do so, however, Russian writers had to adopt rhetorical subterfuges that masked their true targets, and readers adapted by learning to decipher the double-coded allusions to forbidden topics. So, for nearly two hundred years, fictions, ingeniously couched in "Aesopian language," spoke to every political development in the czarist establishment and the world at large. But in Chekhov's little stories, readers looked in vain for allusions to current events and editorial commentary. His tales about ordinary people doing ordinary things in ordinary places offered a stark moral: live fully, simply, with integrity, paying attention to every instant, every sensation, and every interaction.

Chekhov sounded a prophetic retreat from the oracular mission of the writer that had been the earmark of Russian artistic prose. "All great sages are as despotic as generals," he confided to Suvorin. "So to hell with the philosophy of the great men of this world!"[14] Instead, the epistemology on which he built his aesthetics required a vow of humility and a preliminary admission of ignorance. "It is high time for writers, and especially for true artists," insisted Chekhov, "to admit that it's impossible to explain anything. Socrates acknowledged this long ago, as did Voltaire. Only the crowd thinks it knows and understands everything there is to know and understand. And the more stupid it is, the more open-minded it thinks itself to be. But if an artist whom the crowd trusts admits that he understands nothing of what he sees, this fact alone will make a great contribution to the realm of thought and will mark a great step forward."[15] Here, Chekhov's thinking is truly revolutionary, for no other Russian writing before him had pared down the list of prerequisites for authoritative authorial speech to a negative trait: the refusal to claim knowledge in the face of its absence.

A self-made man who worked his way out of the provincial port of Taganrog and a childhood marked by fiscal anxiety and low status, Chekhov was brutally honest in his assessment of self and others.[16] His correspondence and his fiction are testaments to his truth-telling on all subjects—except for his health, about which he was in constant denial. His medical training and his devotion to the principles of the French physician Claude Bernard fed a staunchly materialist realism—and the willingness to call a spade a spade. In a famous letter to his editor Alexei Suvorin, Chekhov articulated the theoretical principle at the basis of his work: "You are confusing two notions, *the solution of a problem* and the *correct posing of the question*. Only the second is essential for the artist."[17] If there was one thing in which Chekhov believed heart and soul it was in the transformative power of heeding this fundamental diagnostic imperative. Four years before his death, he wrote, looking back at his work, "I only wanted to tell people honestly: look, look at how badly you live, how boring are your lives. The important thing is that people should understand this; if they do understand this, they will certainly invent a different and a far better life. Man will become better only once we have shown him as he is."[18]

Russia in the final decades of the nineteenth century was still a nasty, brutish, unforgiving sort of place for someone not born into the aristocracy and thus lacking automatic admission to university study and a high-priced European grand tour, followed by an advantageous marriage and a sinecure in government service. Chekhov relied on himself—in life as well as in his art. He had no use for coteries, cliques, and societies. Moving in and out of literary and social milieus, he was immune to the intellectual fads for which educated, pedigreed Russians had an almost fatal weakness. Populism, socialism, decadence, symbolism, Tolstoy's dogma of nonresistance to evil and adulation of the peasant—all washed off Chekhov's back like so much rain. "I have peasant blood flowing in my veins," Chekhov wrote to Suvorin. "So I am not the one to be impressed by peasant virtues." Nor was he swayed by Tolstoy's fanatical asceticism about the virtue of abstinence from physical pleasures. "My sense of fair play tells me," he wrote, "that there is more love of humanity in steam and electricity than in chastity and abstention from meat."[19]

This pragmatic attachment to comfort and security—what we would call the "bourgeois values"—was only the material side of Chekhov's ethos of existential responsibility. A stoic by conviction and necessity, Chekhov sought a moral calculus by which modern man could live a virtuous and pleasurable life. His ill health in fact provided a constant "reality check" on what was important and what superfluous. Living with the omnipresent awareness of death, the tubercular Chekhov applied the yardstick of mortality to every expenditure of passion, irritation, despair, anguish, pettiness, hard-heartedness, greed, or vanity.

This proto-existential calculation might have struck contemporaries as amoral, but it was entirely consonant with the modern sensibility charted by, among others, Dostoevsky, Nietzsche, and Freud. Theirs too was a universe from which God—the ultimate umpire of right and wrong, good and evil—had been banished. Chekhov, force-fed religion by a tyrannical father, had developed a spiritual allergy to absolutes. Yet he realized that by declaring God dead, modern man had not eliminated the problem of meaning and value; he had only moved its solution to another plane.

Chekhov's stories—even the earliest comic sketches dashed off for money—expose conventional piety as a feeble moral guide with a selective memory, ready to excuse every kind of viciousness in the name of abstractions (Order! Security! Family!). This was, in fact, the moral climate of the closing decades of the nineteenth century, when, exhausted by the legal, social, and economic reforms of Alexander II, Russia slumped into a stultifying inertia of official Orthodoxy and nationalism. Rather than tackling the big political issues, however, Chekhov took his moral crusade into the private lives of individuals. In his view, only the individual personality, unencumbered by dogma, could right the wrongs of a class, a nation, or an age and sow the seeds of genuine historical change. "I believe in particular people, I see salvation in particular personalities, scattered here and there throughout the whole of Russia—whether they are intellectuals or peasants, there is strength in them, though they are few."[20]

# SKEPTIC

A physician with a deep understanding of the material causes of spiritual distress—poverty, malnutrition, poor hygiene, sexual frustration, sleep deprivation—Chekhov asked how one can live with dignity and joy without the Big Overseers of Religion, State, and Ideology looking over one's shoulder. As he famously confided in a letter to Alexei Pleshcheyev, "My holy of holies is the human body, health, intelligence, talent, inspiration, love, and absolute freedom, freedom from violence and falsehood, no matter what form these might take. This is the program to which I would adhere were I a great artist."[21] In an age of creeping agnosticism, when death is the only absolute, Chekhov's protagonists eat, drink, work, court, and carry on trivial conversations between the iron necessity of death and the terrifying freedom to improvise meaning for life. Sentenced to die and powerless to chart the trajectories of their lives (which are usually entirely out of their control), all are shown, in ways subtle and small, as having the freedom to choose how to respond to the challenges and obstacles of the everyday. In a letter to his brother Nikolai, Chekhov sketched out this "gospel" in characteristically concrete terms, avoiding all abstraction:

Educated people, in my opinion, should satisfy the following conditions: They respect the individual, and therefore they are extremely tolerant, gentle, polite, and compliant.... They don't make a fuss about a hammer or a lost galosh.... They forgive noise, cold, overcooked meat, and jokes.... They don't humiliate themselves with the aim of arousing somebody else's sympathy. They don't play on other people's heartstrings so as to be sighed and fussed over in return. They don't say: "Nobody understands me!" or: "I've wasted my talents!" ... They are not vain. They are not interested in such false treasures as acquaintance with celebrities.... They cultivate their aesthetic sense. They are incapable of going to sleep in their clothes, of seeing bedbugs in a crack in the wall, of breathing foul air, of walking on a floor that has been spat on, of eating things cooked on a kerosene stove.[22]

The ethical code formulated in constant mindfulness of death includes aesthetics in a way that is familiar to us. For Chekhov, the good life is inseparable from the beautiful, and both require respect for nature. In his letters and his stories, Chekhov insists on seeing nature as the arena in which the fullness of the human personality can be given its scope. And it is in his characters' regard or disregard for the nonhuman beings of the world—plants and animals—that Chekhov finds the ethical core of individuals. In this respect too, he was prescient of our contemporary commitment to environmental responsibility by promoting the preservation of nature as the touchstone of the moral potential of man. As A. P. Chudakov reminds us, Chekhov "was the first literary figure to include in the ethical sphere man's attitude to nature."[23]

The protagonist of his early play *The Wood-Demon*, a physician by the name of Khrushchov, sounds the clarion call of eco-activism when he protests his neighbor's decision to cut down a forest: "To fell a thousand trees, to destroy them for a couple of thousand rubles, for clothes for your womenfolk, for whims and luxury...[t]o destroy them so that posterity will curse our barbarity!"[24] This sentiment echoes in a number of Chekhov's works—"Gooseberries," *Three Sisters*, *The Cherry Orchard*—in the various iterations that eventually found their way into our environmentalist program. Chekhov's concern for the biosphere stems from a peasant's pragmatism but sounds like the formula for contemporary holistic thinking. For example, the protagonist of an early story notes: "The sun, the sky, the woods, the rivers, the creatures—it was all created, adapted, mutually adjusted. Everything was put in order and knows its place."[25]

# CRAFTSMAN

Chekhov's life fit neatly within the life span of Leo Tolstoy, who preceded him by thirty-two years and outlived him by another six. The elder realist had much to teach the young doctor, but the precocious pupil forged boldly ahead into the faster rhythms, smaller forms, and telegraphic style fit for the coming century of progress, speed, and shortened attention spans. The two squared off like David and Goliath, the miniaturist versus the creator of what Henry James dubbed the "loose baggy monster" of *War and Peace*. Chekhov complained that tendentiousness and prejudice spoiled Tolstoy's prose. Tolstoy, for his part, lamented Chekhov's clinical training as a physician for the same reason. Yet the old man had profound admiration for the younger's achievement. "In Chekhov," Tolstoy wrote, "everything is real to the verge of illusion. His stories give the impression of a stereoscope. He throws words about in an apparent disorder, and, like an impressionist painter, he achieves wonderful results by his touches."[26]

What were the touches that produced this unprecedented realism? His superbly crafted stories are modern because they have the appearance of being under-engineered. They give no answers. They don't insult our intelligence. They don't give short shrift to psychological complexities. They acknowledge the vast importance of the minute, venal things in life—like the pinching shoe and the borborygmi of the belly—as decisive for destiny. Chekhov recrafted the rules of engagement and moved the short story genre into the modern age, handing us a virtually new form, trimmed of its traditional fat and gristle. For one, he abolished the fussy, intrusive, judgmental narrators of the nineteenth century who insinuate themselves between the slice of life held up for scrutiny and the reader's eye. His narrator does not lead us by the hand or tell us when to laugh or cry, decry or applaud. He lets his characters speak their minds, in their own words, no matter how incoherently they may grope for the semblance of a thought. What they fail to say explicitly emerges from the silences, the gaps between words, and from the sparse notation of setting, atmosphere, gesture, and costume.

Chekhov posited an intelligent, independent-minded reader, someone who frankly acknowledges having trouble subscribing to cut-and-dried nostrums, religious frameworks, and conventional cant, who goes to fiction not in order to reinforce pet peeves or confirm what's already known. The Chekhovian reader wants to be challenged to think in unfamiliar ways, to be made uncomfortable, to be stretched and affronted, even bored and disappointed. Life, after all, is like that.

I like to think that if Chekhov's texts were buildings, they would be designed by Le Corbusier rather than by McKim, Mead, and White, the high priests of the frilly, ornamented confections of the Beaux Arts. Chekhov eliminates the frame—not always, to be sure, but generally. The conventional opening gambit of the short story inherited from Boccaccio and his *Decameron* is the narrative situation of a group of friends gathering, under some pretext or another, to exchange stories. Chekhov typically leaps into the thick of the action—or non-action, as the case may be—and trusts us to get our bearings from the subtle signposts he gives us.

He abhors clutter. In a letter to his brother Alexander, Chekhov writes, "There's no need to chase after a crowd of characters. Only two should be at the center of gravity: he and she."[27] His boilerplate advice on revisions is to throw out the first three pages and eliminate clichés, redundancies, and ornament for its own sake. Chekhov's minimalist aesthetic is hard to pull off, because if one goes the route of "less is more," the "less" must derive from a very deep and extensive fund of knowledge. "It's not enough to put words together. One has to know something. One has to work at knowing something. One has to study and have something to say about the world. In short, one needs to be a scientist."

# TEACHER

How relevant is the advice of someone writing over one hundred years ago—and, to make matters worse, in a place with cultural traditions, reading habits, and conventions seriously different from our own? As I have been trying to argue, Chekhov is neither anachronistic nor culturally narrow in his subject matter and in his form. His sublime stories are the best proof that, up against roughly the same pressures, distractions, impediments, and insecurities that we face today, he had a few tricks up his sleeve. Chekhov's life experience is particularly helpful to those of us who also need to blast a hole for writing in the logjams of our lives. His doubled professional life gave him the perfect balance between the potentially claustrophobic isolation that writing requires and the intense and extensive contact with the most diverse personalities and predicaments that medicine affords. As a physician—one pathetically inept at charging and collecting fees—he daily came into contact with the full gamut of human behavior. Every medical intervention became the occasion for a story. By the time he entered the field, medicine, at least as taught by his theoretical mentor Dr. Claude Bernard, had shed its cruder ties to moral and ethical etiology. In other words, rather than moralize overtly or by implication, medical science pathologized life. Throughout Chekhov's life, medicine remained a solid ally in helping him avoid the—to our sensibility—intrusive moralizing of a Dostoevsky or Tolstoy.

And finally, we want Chekhov's advice on writing because we frankly like him. The best sense of the man comes, not surprisingly, from his correspondence with the actress Olga Knipper, whom he courted and married before his death.[28] Her questions to him about his hygiene, dress, eating, sleeping, and working habits reveal a bachelor coddled by an adoring sister and mother; an obsessively gregarious host who could not say no to guests who sapped him of strength and time for his writing; a frail invalid husbanding his dwindling vital energy; a jealous, emotionally reticent lover loath to spill his guts; and a balding man squaring off against middle age by massaging hair tonics into his scalp. Writing came hard to him in his last years, when he challenged himself to write plays that would revolutionize the theater and short stories as terse as haiku.

## WRITING MATTERS

Chekhov had a deep motive for his aesthetic iconoclasm: he believed in the profoundly transformative power of art. Writing matters because, he was convinced, it has an impact on the ways in which we see reality, and by extension, the ways in which we eventually choreograph the relationships and responses in our lives. That is why in matters of craft Chekhov was an obsessive perfectionist who chronically missed deadlines and agonized over every adjective, comma, and semicolon. "In a work of art," he explained, "punctuation often plays the part of musical notation. It demands instinct and experience, not knowledge from a textbook."[29] If his contemporaries found his work disorienting, disturbing, and depressing, it was perhaps because he forced them into the *terra incognita* of a new, utterly modern sensibility that they felt themselves inadequate to enter. "New literary forms always produce new forms of life," he jotted in his notebook. "And that is why they are so revolting to the conservative human mind."[30]

In the end, the advice he gives his fellow writers comes from the "felt fact" of his daily, minute-by-minute struggle to keep writing, to have something worthwhile to say, and to keep living at the same time. What makes him so very attractive as a mentor is that he wants it all: friends, good company, excursions to the country, travel, theater, music, good conversation, family, love, flirtations. He is the master multi-tasker, juggling medicine and writing short stories, plays, and nonfiction. He takes a vital part in the life of his community, pitching in during cholera epidemics, building schools, donating time and talent to philanthropic causes, all the while supporting his parents and siblings. He is always "at home" to guests and patients. Somehow, even with his delicate health, he figures out how to make his art happen. He does not agonize or problematize. As the letters reprinted in this volume will show, he staunchly believes that practice makes perfect. Habit is the engine of success. Good habits produce good results. Being a productive writer is no more complicated than maintaining good hygiene habits. Brush your teeth twice a day and you'll have a healthy mouth. Write an hour a day and you'll have a book.

# HOW TO
# WRITE LIKE
# CHEKHOV

PART ONE: THEORY

## No Plot, No Ending

꩜

# 1
# GENERAL QUESTIONS

⋘⋙

## WHY WRITE?

### Why I Write

*Letter to Maxim Gorky,*[1] *Yalta, January 18, 1899*

Your words about locomotives, rails, and noses getting stuck, are charming but quite unjust. If noses do get stuck it is not because of writing; quite the other way around: writing is the result of sticking one's nose into it and having nowhere else to go.

### Neither for Fame nor Profit

*Letter to Alexei Suvorin,*[2] *Moscow, December 23, 1888*

It makes as much sense to write for [critics] as it does to ask someone suffering from a cold to smell flowers. There are times when I get truly discouraged. For whom and to what end do I write? For the public? But I have never actually seen this public and have less faith in its existence than in ghosts: it is uneducated and bad mannered, and even at its best treats us unscrupulously and insincerely. I have no idea whether this public even needs me. Burenin[3] says that it does not need me and that I am wasting my time, but meanwhile the Academy has awarded me a prize; so, what does it all mean?[4] Is it money I want? But I have never had money, and because I am not used to having any, I am quite indifferent to it. I simply cannot make myself work for money. Is it praise I want? Praise only irritates me. An entire crowd of littérateurs, students, Yevreynov, Pleshcheyev, old maids, etc., heaped praise on my "An Attack of Nerves," but only Grigorovich noticed my description of the first snowfall.[5] Etc. etc. If only we had worthwhile critics, then I could be reassured that I am collecting material—whether good or bad doesn't matter—and that I am as necessary to those who devote themselves to studying life, as a planet is to the astronomer. If this were the case, then I would throw myself into my work and know that it has a purpose. As things stand now, however, you, Muravlin, some other kindred spirits, and I are like madmen writing books and plays for nothing more than our own pleasure.[6] One's pleasure, to be sure, is a fine thing: one feels it as long as one's writing, but what about when one's done writing? What then? ...Entire populations, religions, languages, and cultures have vanished without a trace because there were no historians or biologists to record their existence. In precisely the same way scores of lives and works of art are disappearing right before our eyes because there is absolutely no criticism.

## On Gaiety and Gloomy Tales

*Letter to Lydia Avilova,*[7] *Nice, October 6, 1897*

You complain that my characters are gloomy. This, alas, is not my fault! That is just how they turn out, without my doing it on purpose, and while I am writing, it never occurs to me that I might be depressing. At any rate, while I am working I am always in a good mood. It has been said that gloomy, melancholy people always write in a cheery way, whereas cheery people turn out writing that always manages to induce gloom. I, you see, have a joyous disposition; or, at least, I have spent the first thirty years of my life having fun, as they say.

## The Laws of Nature

*Letter to Alexandra Khotyaintseva,*[8] *Nice, November 26, 1897*

I have noticed still another law of nature: the more fun I am having, the more depressing my stories turn out.

## The Desire to Write, the Desire to Live

*Letter to Alexander Chekhov, Melikhovo,*[9] *April 15, 1894*

I do not feel like writing, and besides, it is difficult to combine the desire to live with the desire to write.

# FOR WHOM SHOULD ONE WRITE?

## Forget Yourself

*Letter to Alexander Chekhov, Moscow, February 20, 1883*

All you need to do is be more honest with yourself: throw yourself overboard into everything, everywhere; do not make yourself the hero of your own novel; forget yourself—if only for half an hour. You have written a story in which a young married couple spends an entire dinner doing nothing but kissing, whining, and talking baby talk....They do not say a single sensible thing, just *sweet nothings!* You did not write this for the reader...you wrote this because *you yourself* enjoy this silly chatter. If, on the other hand, you were to describe the dinner, how they ate, what they ate, what the cook looked like; if you were to show your hero's vulgarity, the satisfaction he takes in his own idle happiness, and the vulgarity of your heroine, in all the ridiculousness of her love for that overstuffed, overfed, napkin-festooned goose of a husband.... To be sure, everyone likes to see well-fed, contented people, but to describe them one must do more than tell us what *they* talk about and how many times they kiss.... Something else is needed here: a distance from that entirely personal impression that the happiness of newlyweds always makes on those who have not yet turned cynical.... Subjectivity is a terrible thing. If for no other reason, it is terrible because it gives away the novice writer in all his shortcomings.

## The Writer's Audience

*Letter to Alexei Suvorin, Moscow, December 26, 1888*

You say one should not write for critics, but for the public, and that it is too early for me to start complaining. I would like to think, of course, that I am in fact working for the public, but how do I know that is what I am actually doing? I myself get no satisfaction from my work—maybe because it is trivial or for some other reason. The public (please note that I did not call it "base"), in the meantime, treats us dishonestly and insincerely and will never tell us the truth, so there's actually no way of knowing whether it needs me or not. While it might be too early for me to complain, it is never too early to ask whether what I am doing is serious work or just a game. The critics say nothing, the public lies, and my own sense tells me I am wasting my time on nonsense. Am I complaining? I do not remember the tone of my letter, but if I am complaining, I am doing it not just for myself, but also for all our writing brethren, for whom I feel infinite pity.

## For My Contemporaries

*Letter to Dmitry Grigorovich, January 12, 1888*

For my debut in the thick journals,[10] I have chosen the steppe, which has not been described for a long time.... All my pages have come out compact, as though condensed; impressions crowd one atop the other, pile up, squeeze up against each other; the scenes or, as you call them, the flashes, are jammed up against each other, without a break, and so are quite fatiguing. The general effect is not of a picture but of a dry, detailed catalog of impressions, something like an outline; instead of giving the reader an artistic, integrated picture of the steppe, I produce an "encyclopedia of the steppe." The first try is a flop. However, I am not discouraged. Who knows, even an encyclopedia might come in handy. Perhaps it might open the eyes of my contemporaries and show them the wealth and rich veins of beauty that still remain untouched and the boundless scope still open to the Russian artist. If my little tale reminds my colleagues of the steppe they have forgotten; if even one of the motifs I have lightly and roughly sketched prompts some poet, however insignificant, to think, that will be all the reward I need. You, I know, will understand my steppe and for its sake will be willing to forgive the sins I have unintentionally committed. My sins are unintentional because, as I am only now beginning to understand, I *do not yet know how* to write longer pieces.

### Know Your Own Readers

*Letter to Maxim Gorky, Moscow, June 27, 1899*[11]

You plan to walk across Russia? I wish you a pleasant journey, all the best, although it does strike me that as long as you're still hale and hearty, you might be better off studying the people who actually read your work rather than spending a couple of years walking or riding third-class carriages.

If, afterwards, you still feel like taking that walk, by all means, go.

## Writing for Connoisseurs

*Letter to Yakov Polonsky, Moscow, January 18, 1888*

By the way, I am just now at work on a long story that will probably appear in the *Northern Herald*.[12] In my novella, I describe the steppe, the people of the steppe, the birds, the nights, storms, etc. I'm enjoying the work, but I do worry that because I lack experience in writing long pieces my tone might be inconsistent, I grow tired, I don't say everything that needs to be said, and I am not being serious enough. There are many passages that my critics and my readers will not understand, will find trivial, undeserving of attention; but I take pleasure in anticipating that these same passages will be understood and appreciated by two or three literary connoisseurs, and that is enough for me. Overall, however, my little novella does not come up to my expectations. It is clunky, tedious, and too specialized. For today's readers a topic such as the steppe, with its natural landscape and its people, is too specialized and insignificant.

## WHAT TO WRITE, HOW TO WRITE

### How *Not* to Write

> *From* The Notebooks of Doctor Chekhov, *p. 125*

Spare me, Lord, from judging or talking about things I do not know and do not understand!

### Without Plot or Ending

> *Letter to Alexander Chekhov, Babkino, June 16, 1887*

Congratulations on your debut in the *New Times*.[13] However, tell me why you did not pick a serious subject? Your form is splendid, but your characters are wooden, and your subject is trite. Any ol' hi skooler coudov dun betta.... You should take something ordinary, something from everyday life, without a plot or ending.

### The Banalities of Daily Life

> *Letter to Alexei Suvorin, Moscow, December 18, 1893*

Potapenko's play enjoyed modest success.[14] The play does have a certain something, but this something is lost in the clutter of various absurd, extraneous elements (such as, for example, the medical consultation, which is ludicrously unrealistic) and declamations with a Shakespearean flavor. Ukrainians are a mulish lot; they are impressed with the magnificence of their own pronouncements and value their sublime Ukrainian truths to such an extent that they are prepared to sacrifice artistic verisimilitude and even common sense. There is even a saying for this, "The torch of truth burns the hand which bears it." The most successful was the second act: here the banalities of daily life did manage to break through the magniloquence and high-falutin' truths.

## Reading, Watching, Listening

*Letter to Alexei Suvorin, Moscow, March 9, 1890*

Apropos *Sakhalin*...I want to write at least one or two hundred pages and thereby pay off some of my debt to medicine, toward which, as you know, I have behaved like a pig. I may not actually end up writing anything, but even so, the journey will not have lost any of its allure. By reading, watching, and listening I will have discovered and learned a great deal. I have not even left yet, but thanks to the books I've had to read I have learned much about things that everyone should know under penalty of forty lashes and that I've been too ignorant to not learn earlier.

## All Kinds of Subjects

*Letter to Maria Kiselyova,*[15] *Moscow, September 29, 1886*

Write about all kinds of subjects: funny, pathetic, good, bad. Send [me] your stories, drafts, anecdotes, jokes, puns, etc. etc.

## Don't Polish

*Letter to Alexander Chekhov, Moscow, April 11, 1889*

Don't smooth out the rough edges, don't polish; be clumsy and bold. Brevity is the sister of talent.


## It's Not *What* I Saw, but *How* I Saw

*Letter to Alexei Suvorin, SS Baikal, Tartar Strait, September 11, 1890*

I saw *everything*, so it is not a question of *what* I saw, but *how* I saw.


## Cut Mercilessly

*Letter to Alexei Suvorin, Moscow, February 6, 1889*

My soul is filled with sloth and sense of freedom. This is my blood rushing to meet spring. However, I keep working. I am preparing material for my third volume. I am cutting mercilessly. A strange thing has happened: I have developed a mania for brevity. No matter what I read—my own or others' writing—everything strikes me as too long.


## Literary Police

*Letter to Maria Kiselyova, Moscow, January 14, 1887*

There is no police force that could consider itself competent in the sphere of literature. I do agree: what with all the phonies constantly worming their way into literature, it is impossible to give up the muzzle and the knout. However, any way you look at it, there is no better literary police than the critic and the conscience of the author.

## Brevity

*Letter to Alexander Chekhov, Moscow, January 4, 1886*

Do not give anyone permission to shorten or revise your stories.... It is hard to withhold permission; it is a lot easier to resort to the handy expedient of cutting and trimming as *ne plus ultra* as possible and making your own revisions. The more you cut, the more your stories will be published.... But the most important thing of all is to stay sharp, alert, and hot on your task, rewriting five times if need be, cutting, etc., and keeping in mind that all Petersburg is watching the work of the brothers Chekhov.

## Witness, Don't Judge

*Letter to Alexei Suvorin, Sumy, May 30, 1888*

In my opinion, it is not the writer's job to solve such problems as the existence of God, pessimism, etc. The job of the artist is only to record who under which circumstances said or thought what about God or pessimism. The artist must not judge his characters or their words; he must only be an impartial witness. I overhear two Russians carry on a muddled, inconclusive discussion on pessimism; I am duty bound to transmit this conversation exactly as I heard it. Evaluating it is a job for the jury, that is, for the reader. My job demands only one thing of me: to be talented, that is, to distinguish between relevant and irrelevant evidence; to illuminate characters, and to speak in their language. Shcheglov-Leontyev criticizes me for ending one of my stories with the sentence, "You can't really explain why things happen in this world." In his opinion, the writer who is a psychologist *must* explain, otherwise he has no right to call himself a psychologist. I disagree. It is high time for writers—and especially for true artists—to admit that it is impossible to explain anything. Socrates acknowledged this long ago, as did Voltaire. Only the crowd thinks it knows and understands everything there is to know and understand. And the more stupid it is, the more open-minded it thinks itself to be. But if an artist whom the crowd trusts admits that he understands nothing of what he sees, this fact alone will make a great contribution to the realm of thought and will mark a great step forward.

## From Dream to Story

*Letter to Alexei Suvorin, Melikhovo, January 25, 1894*

I wrote "The Black Monk" not under the sway of melancholy, but in a state of perfectly sober reflection.[16] I just felt like giving a picture of megalomania. The image of the monk floating across the field came to me in a dream, and when I woke up in the morning, I told Misha[17] about it. So please tell Anna Ivanovna[18] that poor Anton Pavlovich has, thank God, not yet lost his mind, and that he eats too much at dinner and consequently sees monks in his dreams.

# Art Should Not Solve Problems

*Letter to Alexei Suvorin, Moscow, October 27, 1888*

I do sometimes preach heresies, but I have never, not once, gone so far as to deny that hard questions have no place in art. In conversations with my fellow writers, I always insist that it is not the job of the artist to solve narrowly specialized questions. It is bad for the artist to tackle what he does not understand. We have specialists for dealing with specialized questions; it is their job to make decisions about the peasant commune, the fate of capitalism, the evils of alcoholism, about boots, and female complaints.... The artist must pass judgment only on what he understands; his sphere of expertise is as limited as that of any other specialist—that's what I keep repeating and advocating. Anyone who says that the artist's sphere leaves no room for questions, but deals exclusively with answers, has never done any writing or done anything with imagery. The artist observes, selects, guesses, and arranges; every one of these operations presupposes a question at its outset. If he has not asked himself a question at the start, he has nothing to guess and nothing to select....

You are right to demand that an author be conscious of what he is doing, but you are confusing two concepts: *solving the problem* and *correctly formulating the problem*. Only the latter is required of the artist. Not a single problem is resolved in *Anna Karenina* or *Eugene Onegin*, and yet the novels satisfy you completely because all the problems they raise are formulated correctly.[19] It is the duty of the law courts to correctly formulate problems, but it is up to the members of the jury to solve them, each to his own taste.

## Drawing Life Truthfully

*Letter to Alexei Pleshcheyev, Moscow, April 9, 1889*

My novel made a significant leap forward then ran aground while waiting for the tide to turn.[20] I am dedicating it to you—but I have already written you about this. As the basis of my novel I am taking the lives of some good people: their personalities, their actions, words, thoughts, and hopes; my goal is to kill two birds with one stone: to draw life truthfully and at the same time to show the extent to which this life deviates from the norm. The norm is inaccessible to me, as it is to every one of us. We know what a dishonorable act is, but we have no idea what honor itself might be. I intend to keep to a framework that is close to my heart and tested by people who are stronger and cleverer than I am.

## Socrates and the Cook

*Letter to Alexei Suvorin, Melikhovo, January 2, 1894*

It is easier to write about Socrates than about a young lady or a cook.

# WHEN AND HOW MUCH TO WRITE

## Wait a Year

*Letter to Elena Shavrova,*[21] *Melikhovo, February 28, 1895*

You are right: it is a risky topic.[22] I cannot tell you anything definite, but I can only advise you to lock up the story in a trunk and keep it there for a year: only then should you read it over.

## The Author's Warehouse

*Letter to Alexei Suvorin, Moscow, October 27, 1888*

My conscience tells me that, even though I did receive the prize,[23] my literary career has not even begun yet. The plots for five novellas and two novels are languishing in my head. One of the novels was conceived so long ago that several of the characters have already grown old and out of date even before they had a chance to take form on paper. There is an entire army of people in my head begging to get out and just waiting for my command. Everything I have written to this point is rubbish in comparison with what I would want to have written and what I would be thrilled to be writing.... I do not like the fact that I am successful; the plots that are still in my head are fretting with jealous irritation over the ones I have already put down in writing. It annoys me to think that all the stuff that is nonsense is already written up while the good material is still sitting around in the warehouse like un-sold inventory. Of course, there is a lot of exaggeration in my whining, and there is also a lot that is nothing more than *my impression*, but there is also a dole—a sizable dole—of truth. What do I mean by a sizeable dole? The images that I feel are among the best, that I love and jealously hoard rather than waste or butcher in a rush job on some "Name Day Party" or other."[24]... If my love is a mistake, then I am wrong, but it is also entirely possible that it is not a mistake! Either I am an idiot and a conceited fool, or I am an organism capable of becoming a good writer. Everything I am writing at present bores me and leaves me indifferent, but everything that is still only in my head interests me, moves me, and excites me. From all of this I have concluded that everyone else is on the wrong track and I am the only one who knows the secret of what needs to be done. This is probably what most writers think. Anyhow, these are the kinds of issues that would drive the devil himself crazy.

## Five or Six Days

*Letter to Alexander Lazarev-Gruzinsky,*[25]
*Moscow, March 13, 1890*

To write a story you need five or six days, during which time you must be thinking about it every moment, otherwise you will never be able to frame good sentences. Before it reaches the page, every sentence must spend two days in the brain, lying perfectly still and putting on weight. It goes without saying, of course, that I am too lazy to mind my own rule, but I do recommend it to you young writers, all the more so because I have experienced its beneficent results firsthand

and know that the rough drafts of all true artists are a mess of deletions and corrections, marked up from top to bottom in a patchwork of cuts and insertions that are themselves re-crossed out and mangled.

## A Year and Six Months

*Letter to Lydia Avilova, St. Petersburg, February 15, 1895*

Write your novel. Work on writing it for one year. Then spend half a month cutting it, and only after that should you have it published. As it is, you spend too little time detailing your work, whereas a writer should not so much write as embroider on paper; the work should be painstaking, laborious.

## Deadlines

*Letter to Alexei Suvorin, Moscow, February 21, 1886*

I write relatively little: no more than two or three very short stories per week. I will find a way to make time for writing for the *New Times*, but am glad that meeting deadlines is not one of your preconditions for my publishing in your paper. Deadlines produce haste and the feeling of a great weight pressing down on my neck, and both of these get in the way of writing.... Personally, deadlines do not work for me for the simple reason that I am a physician and am practicing medicine.... I cannot promise that tomorrow I might not have to spend the entire day away from my writing desk.... This is why there is always a danger that I will miss a deadline and fall behind schedule.

## Never Rush

*Letter to Alexei Pleshcheyev, Moscow, April 9, 1888*

In any case, please let Anna Mikhailovna [Evreinova][26] know that if I am in no rush to deliver on my promise, it is only because I am not pleased with my work. I will send it just as soon as I am satisfied or almost satisfied.... I would send her the story now, but I really do not think it would be wise to rush. I am by nature cautious and suspicious; I am afraid to rush, and in general I am afraid to publish. I am always worrying that people will tire of me and I will turn into one of those ballast generators on the order of a Yasinsky, or Mamin, or Bazhin, etc., who, like myself, "had once inspired great hopes."[27] This fear of mine is well founded: I have been publishing for a long time now, with around two hundred pounds of stories in print, but even at this late date I really cannot say I know my strengths and weaknesses.

# 2

# SPECIFIC QUESTIONS

❧

## TRUTH

### Six Conditions

*Letter to Alexander Chekhov, Moscow, May 10, 1886*

"The City of the Future" is a magnificent theme, new and interesting. If you do not get lazy, I think you will write a decent story, but damn it, you are such a lazybones! "The City of the Future" will be a work of art only on the condition that it have: (1) no politico-socio-economic logorrheic eruptions; (2) absolute objectivity; (3) truthful representation of characters and objects; (4) maximal conciseness; (5) boldness and originality; no clichés; (6) sincerity.

### Neither Cosmetician nor Entertainer

*Letter to Maria Kiselyova, Moscow, January 14, 1887*

Your observation that the world "swarms with villains and villainesses" is correct. Human nature is imperfect, so it would be odd to show only the righteous elements. And to imagine that literature has the charge of picking the "pearls" out of a heap of scoundrels is tantamount to negating literature altogether. Literature is included among the arts because it depicts life as it actually exists. Its aim is truth—unconditional and honest. It would be as perilous to restrict its function to something so specialized as digging for "pearls" as it would be to require Levitan[1] to paint a tree without including its dirty bark or yellowing leaves. I agree that a "pearl" is a very fine thing, but a writer, after all, is not a confectioner, nor a cosmetician, nor an entertainer. He is a human being who is contractually bound to honor his sense of duty and to follow the dictates of his conscience. Once in, he cannot back out; no matter how appalled he might be, he must overcome his squeamishness and be willing to dirty his imagination in the muck of life.... He is just like any ordinary journalist. What would you say if out of squeamishness or a desire to please his readers a journalist were to write only about honest politicians, high-minded ladies, and virtuous railroad men?

To a chemist nothing in the world is impure. The writer must be just as objective as the chemist; he must free himself of everyday subjectivity, and he must know that manure plays a most respectable role in nature and that evil passions are just as much a part of life as virtues.

## Facts and Artistic Conventions

*Letter to Grigory Rossolimo, Yalta, October 11, 1899*

There is no doubt in my mind that my medical work has had a serious impact on my writing; it has significantly broadened the scope of my observations and enriched me with knowledge whose value for me as a writer only a fellow physician can appreciate. It has also served as a guiding principle in my art; my intimacy with medicine has probably helped me avoid many mistakes. My familiarity with the natural sciences and the scientific method has always kept me on my guard. I have tried to be consistent with scientific data wherever possible—and where this was impossible, I have preferred not writing at all. Let me note, in this regard, that art does not always allow for total agreement with scientific data; death by poison cannot be represented onstage as it actually occurs in real life. However, some conformity with scientific facts should be perceptible even within the framework of artistic conventions. In other words, the reader or the spectator should be able to perceive that an artistic convention is at work, but also that the author is fully aware of the reality of the situation he is representing.

## An Example

*Letter to Alexei Suvorin, Moscow, October 25, 1891*

Had I been treating Prince Andrei,[2] I would have cured him. I find it bizarre to read that the wound of the Prince, a wealthy man in the constant care of a physician and nursed by Natasha and Sonya, should have given off the stench of a corpse. What a nasty business medicine was in those days. While writing his tremendous novel, Tolstoy must certainly have been filled with an unconscious hatred for medicine.

## Do Not Invent Sufferings You Have Not Experienced Yourself

*Letter to Alexander Chekhov, Moscow, April 6, 1886*

Where in the world did you find the married couple in your story that you have discussing scholarly articles over dinner…and where in heaven's name are these scholarly articles supposed to exist? For God's sake, have some self-respect and do not run off at the mouth if your brain is out to lunch. Do not write more than two stories a week, work on shortening and polishing them, and make your work count. Do not invent sufferings you have not experienced yourself, and do not describe scenes you have not witnessed yourself: a falsehood is much more tedious in a story than in a conversation....

Bear in mind—every single moment—that your pen and your talent will be much more useful to you in the future than they are now, so do not profane them. Write, but keep a watchful eye on every line lest you slip up.... And note, that since you are not burdened with deadlines, you are able to devote several evenings to a single small piece.

# No Lying in Art

*Undated letter [1900?]*[3]

One must never lie. Art has this great specification: it simply does not tolerate falsehood. One can lie in love, politics, and medicine: one can mislead the public or even God; but there is absolutely no lying in art.

# Do Not Lie to Yourself

*Letter to Alexei Suvorin, Melikhovo, November 25, 1892*

Just remember that the writers we call "eternal" or just plain "good" and who intoxicate us, share one very important trait: they are all moving toward some definite point and they summon us to follow and make us comprehend—not just with our mind, but with our entire being—that they have a precise goal, just as in the case of Hamlet's father, whose ghost had a motive for coming and stirring Hamlet's imagination. Depending on their caliber, some have very concrete goals—such as serfdom, the liberation of their motherland, politics, beauty, or simply vodka, as in the case of Denis Davydov[4]; others have more abstract objectives— God, life beyond death, the well-being of humanity, etc. The very best among them are realistic and depict life as it is, but because each life is permeated with a consciousness of its own goal, you feel life not only as it is but also as it should be, and this captivates you. And what about us? Us! We depict life as it is: period. Beat us, whip us, you will not get us to budge. We have no other goals, short- or long-range: you will not find a thing in our souls. We have no politics; we do not believe in revolution; there is no God; we have no fear of ghosts; and as for me—I am not afraid even of death or blindness. One who wants nothing, hopes for nothing, and fears nothing cannot be an artist. Maybe this is a sickness, though it really does not matter what you call it. The crucial thing is to realize that this is a critical situation. I cannot predict what will happen to us in ten or twenty years. Maybe something will change, but for now you would be rash to expect anything genuinely worthwhile from us, no matter how talented we might be. We write mechanically, bowing to the long-established order that mandates some serve in the bureaucracy, others in commerce, still others in letters.... You and Grigorovich[5] find me to be intelligent. Yes, I am intelligent, at least intelligent enough to not hide my illness from myself or lie to myself or cover up my own emptiness with other people's rags.

## Rid Yourself of Violence and Falsehood

*Letter to Alexei Pleshcheyev, Moscow, October 4, 1888*

I am not a liberal, a conservative, a gradualist, a monk, or an indifferentist. I would like to be a free artist and nothing else, and regret that God has not given me the strength to be one. I hate falsehood and violence in all their forms, and reserve the same loathing for provincial secretaries, Notovich, and Gradovsky.[6] Pharisaism, stupidity, and arbitrariness reign not only in the homes of merchants and in police stations. I see them in science, in literature, in the younger generation....

For this reason I have no partiality for policemen, butchers, scientists, writers, or the younger generation. My holy of holies is the human body, health, intelligence, talent, inspiration, love, and absolute freedom, freedom from violence and falsehood, no matter what form these might take. This is the program to which I would adhere were I a great artist.

# DESCRIPTIONS

## I Limit Myself to Describing

*Letter to Dmitry Grigorovich, Moscow, October 9, 1888*

I have not yet acquired a political, religious, or philosophical worldview; I change my views every day and consequently have to confine myself to describing how my protagonists love, marry, breed, die, and talk.

## Try Not to Tire the Reader

*Letter to Alexander Zhirkevich,[7] Melikhovo, April 2, 1895*

Routine descriptions: "The étagère against the wall sparkled with books." Why not simply say, "the bookshelf"? You write that the volumes of Pushkin are "disconnected from each other," that the "Inexpensive Library" edition is "squashed." What is the point? You are only distracting and tiring the reader by forcing him to stop and reconstruct in his imagination the sparkling étagère and the squashed *Hamlet*. That's problem number one. Problem number two is that all these descriptions are complicated, mannered, and stale. Nowadays only ladies might write, "the poster pro-claimed" or "a face framed by hair."

## Smell the Bagels

*Letter to Maxim Gorky, Yalta, February 15, 1900*

"Twenty-Six Men and a Girl"[8] is a fine story, the best among the pieces published in *Life*, that dilettante journal. In your story one can feel the place, smell the bagels.

## Smell the Summer

*Letter to Alexei Pleshcheyev, Moscow, February 3, 1888*

"The Steppe" is finished and in the mail. There was barely enough for a nickel, and now, suddenly, there is almost enough to make a dollar. I started out with the intention of writing thirty or forty pages at most, and ended up with close to eighty. I am worn out and exhausted from the unfamiliar strain of writing at such length; it was hard going, and I feel that I have written a lot of nonsense.

Please be indulgent!

The actual subject matter of "The Steppe" is not important; if the story shows even modest success, I will use it as the basis for a much longer novella and will develop it further. You will not find a single character here that deserves close attention or further elaboration.

While I was writing, I had the feeling that I could actually smell the summer and the steppe. How good it would be to go there!

...My "Steppe" is actually less like a story than an encyclopedia of the steppe.

## The Smell of Hay

*Letter to Dmitry Grigorovich, Moscow, January 12, 1888*
For my debut in the "thick journal," I have selected the steppe, which no one has described for some time now. I describe the expanse, the lilac horizon, the shepherds,...the storms at night, the wayside inns, the wagon trains, the birds of the steppe, and so on. Each chapter is its own story, and all the chapters are as intimately connected and joined as the five figures in a quadrille. I am trying to give them a common note and a common tone, which I have a better chance of achieving by having a single character that runs through all the chapters. I feel that I have managed to work through quite a few issues, and there are passages that give off the smell of hay.

## Feeling with Your Hands

*Letter to Maxim Gorky, Yalta, December 3, 1898*
You ask what I think of your stories. What do I think? That you have talent is beyond doubt, as is the fact that this is a genuine, major talent. It shows up with tremendous force, for example, in your story "In the Steppe," and it actually made me jealous that you had written it instead of me. You are an artist and an intelligent man. You have an extraordinary feel for reality. You are plastic, i.e., when you are

describing something you are actually seeing it and feeling it with your hands. This is true art.

## Descriptions of Nature: Details

*Letter to Alexander Chekhov, Moscow, May 19, 1886*

I think that descriptions of nature should be short and to the point. Commonplaces such as, "The setting sun bathing in the waves of the darkening sea poured out a flood of crimson gold," etc., and, "The swallows skimming the surface of the water chirped joyously"—such commonplaces should be eliminated. In describing nature, focus on minute details and group them in such a way that when the reader will have finished reading, he will be able to close his eyes and see a complete picture. You can produce the impression of a moonlit night, for example, by writing that the broken bottle glass twinkled like stars on the milldam, and that the black shadow of a dog or a wolf rolled by, and so on. Nature appears to be animated if you are not afraid to use comparisons between natural phenomena and human actions.

## Descriptions of Nature: Simplicity

*Letter to Maxim Gorky, Yalta, January 3, 1899*

Your nature descriptions are artistic; you are a true landscape painter. However, your frequent comparisons to humans (anthropomorphism)—the sea breathes, the sky looks on, the steppe basks in the sun, nature whispers, speaks, weeps, and so on—these kinds of personifications make your descriptions somewhat monotonous, a touch saccharine, vague; in descriptions of nature, vibrancy and expressivity are best produced by simple techniques, for example: using simple phrases such as "the sun set," "it got dark," "it started to rain," and so on. This kind of simplicity distinguishes your work to a much greater degree than it does other writers.

## Descriptions of Nature: Less Is More

*Letter to Alexander Zhirkevich, Melikhovo, April 2, 1895*
The story should begin with the sentence, "Somov, it seems, was upset." Everything that comes before—that stuff about the cloud prostrating itself, about the sparrows, the field stretching out into the distance—all these elements are just so much tribute paid to routine. You do have a feeling for nature, but you do not describe it the way you feel it. Descriptions of nature should first of all be visual, so that when the reader closes his eyes, he can immediately imagine the landscape that was just described; an inventory of such elements as dusk, a leaden shade of gray, puddle, damp, silvery poplars, cloud-specked horizon, sparrows, distant woods—does not a picture make because no matter how hard I try, I just can't imagine the pieces into a coherent whole. I think that in stories such as yours, descriptions of nature are appropriate and do not ruin the effect only when they help communicate a mood, the way music does in a melodeclamation. In passages such

as the ones where reveille is sounding and soldiers are singing "Our Father," where the commander is returning to the battalion at night, and when in the morning the soldier is being taken to be punished—in these passages, your landscape works perfectly and you are a master. The flashes of heat lightning are effective; but you need have mentioned them only once, as if accidentally, without calling attention to them: otherwise, you weaken the impression and break the reader's mood.

## Descriptions of Emotional States

*Letter to Alexander Chekhov, Moscow, May 19, 1886*

The psychological sphere also demands details. Spare us commonplaces, for God's sake. Best of all, avoid describing the emotional states of your protagonists; one should try to make these apparent from their actions.

## Details

*Letter to Elena Shavrova, Serpukhov, November 22, 1894*

If it's weaknesses you want, then allow me to point out one that you repeat in all your stories: the foreground of your descriptions is taken up with a mass of details. You are an excellent observer. You hate to part with details, but what can one do? One must sacrifice them for the sake of the whole. The reason for this is physical: one must write and remember that details, even very interesting details, exhaust the reader's attention.

## No Tie and an Unbuttoned Waistcoat

*Letter to Alexander Lazarev-Gruzinsky,*
*Moscow, October 20, 1888*

Your nature descriptions are not at all bad: it is a good thing that you are afraid of the superficial and the conventional. However, you are not giving free rein to your temperament. As a result, your devices lack originality. You should describe women in such a way that the reader will have the impression you have taken off your tie and unbuttoned your waistcoat; the same goes for your nature descriptions. Give yourself a little freedom.

# CHARACTERS

## Number of Characters

*Letter to Alexander Chekhov, Moscow, May 19, 1886*

There is no need to chase after a crowd of characters. Only two should be at the center of gravity: he and she.

## Focus on Two Principals

*Letter to Dmitry Grigorovich, Moscow, October 9, 1888*

All the ideas, all the women, men, and nature scenes that I have collected for a novel will remain safe and sound. I promise you, I will not squander them on trivia. The novel covers several families and a district—with all its forests, rivers, ferries, and railroad. In the district, the focus will be on the two principals, one male and one female, and all the other pawns will be grouped around them.

## Superfluous Characters

*Letter to Elena Shavrova, Melikhovo, February 28, 1895*

The story is a little thin: it's got the musty smell of a sermon, the details run out in all directions like spilled oil, the characters are indistinguishable one from the other. Some characters—the heroine's brother, for example, or her mother—are superfluous. Some episodes are superfluous: for example, the events and the conversations before the wedding, and, for that matter, everything that has to do with the wedding.

## Living Characters

*Letter to Alexander Chekhov, Babkino, August 2, 1887*

Like all your female characters, Olya does not work. You positively do not know women. My dear soul, you cannot stick to just one type of female character for all eternity. Aside from your high school days, when and where did you come across women like Olya? Would it not be far more intelligent and creative to pair up that magnificent Tartar or Papa with a likable, flesh-and-blood woman rather than that mannequin? That Olya of yours is an insult to the sort of grand portraiture of your "Lighthouse." Not to mention the fact that she is a vague and muddy puppet in contrast to your other characters and in their company makes the same impression as a pair of wet, muddy boots next to a row of polished shoes. For God's sake, not one of your stories has a single female character that is a human being; all your women are some sorts of twitching custards chattering in the language of spoiled vaudeville ingénues.... Revise and do not publish in the *New Times* until you make sure you have produced living characters and you are not falsifying reality.

## Figures and Background

*Letter to Alexei Suvorin, Moscow, October 27, 1888*

I start writing the story on September 10 with the idea of finishing by October 5 at the very latest. If I miss the deadline, I will have broken my word and end up with no money. I begin calmly, un-self-consciously, but somewhere along the middle, I start to get nervous and start worrying the story might be getting too long. I remember that the *Northern Herald* does not have a lot of money and that I am one of its more expensive contributors. This is why the beginning always seems more promising, as if I were writing a novel; the middle is a timid jumble, and the end is an explosion of fireworks, just like a brief sketch. Like it or not, when you're putting a story together, you first worry about the framework: from a crowd of heroes and quasi-heroes you pick out a single figure—a wife or a husband—and you place that figure against a background and then you develop and accentuate it. The rest of the characters you scatter across the background like so much small change, and then you end up with something like a night sky: one big moon in the center of a crowd of very tiny stars. But the moon does not work because it can only make sense if the stars make sense, and meanwhile the stars are not clearly enough worked out…. So what should I do? I do not know. I just do not know. I will just have to trust in the healing power of time.

## Figures and Crowds

*Letter to Maxim Gorky, Yalta, February 9, 1900*

You need to see more, know more, and broaden the scope of what you know. You have an imagination with a long reach and a powerful grasp, but it is like a big oven that never gets enough kindling. This comes across in all your work, but especially so in your stories. You've got two or three characters in your story, but they stand apart from the rest of the crowd. What is obvious is that these characters—and only these characters—have come alive in your imagination, while the crowd somehow remains untouched. I make an exception for your Crimean pieces ("My Fellow Traveler," for instance), where one has a sense not only of the main figures, but also of the human crowd from which they emerge, and of the air, the background, in short—of the whole.

## Mocking the Characters

*Letter to Alexei Suvorin, Melikhovo, February 24, 1893*

Aside from Bazarov's old mother…and mothers in general— and especially the society ladies who, incidentally, are all alike (Liza's mother, Elena's mother), and Lavretsky's mother, a former serf girl, and the simple peasant women—all of

Turgenev's women and girls are unbearably artificial and, forgive me, false.[9] Liza and Elena are not Russian girls, but some sort of pontificating Pythian priestesses overflowing with pretensions entirely beyond their station in life. Irina in *Smoke*, Odintsova in *Fathers and Sons*, and all those torrid, appetizing, insatiable, eternally questing lionesses are total nonsense. Just recall Tolstoy's Anna Karenina, and you will send all of Turgenev's young ladies, seductive shoulders and all, straight to hell. By contrast, Turgenev's negative female types—the ones he caricatures (Kukshina) or mocks (in his ballroom scenes)—are strikingly rendered and could not be more to the point.

## Local Officials

*Letter to Maxim Gorky, Yalta, January 3, 1899*

Never write about *zemstvo* officials.[10] Nothing is easier than writing about obnoxious officials. Readers just love this topic—but these are only the most disagreeable, the most untalented sorts of readers.

## Female Characters

*Letter to Vladimir Korolenko, Moscow, January 9, 1888*

Your "Sakhalin Fugitive,"[11] I think, is the most outstanding work to appear of late.... In your book you are such a solid artist, such a powerhouse that even your most prominent shortcomings pass unnoticed, though they would be the undoing of any lesser artist. For instance, I only just recently nosed out the fact that in your entire book female characters are stubbornly missing.

## Doctors and Patients

*Letter to Elena Shavrova, Melikhovo, February 28, 1895*

I also think that it is not the job of the artist to take people to task for being sick. After all, am I to blame if I have a migraine? Is Sidor to blame for coming down with S,[12] for being more susceptible to it than Taras? Is Akulina to blame for the tuberculosis in her bones? No one is to blame, but even if someone were, then it would be the health officials and not the artists.

The physicians in your story behave abominably. You make them forget doctor-patient confidentiality; what's more, you have them force a seriously ill and paralyzed patient to travel to town.... And the ladies in your story regard S as if it were the devil incarnate. That is not right. S is not a vice, it is not the result of malice: it is a disease, and those suffering from S need warm, compassionate care. It is wrong for a wife to desert her sick husband with the excuse that he has a contagious or revolting sickness. Of course, she can regard S any way she chooses, but the author is obliged to be humane to the very tips of his fingers.

Incidentally, do you know that influenza ravages the organism in ways that are far from insignificant? There are quite a few things in nature than are harmful and hereditary. Even breathing can be harmful. For myself personally I stand by the following rule: I write about patients only if they are characters or if they contribute something vivid to the description. I am afraid of scaring people with illnesses.

## Successes and Failures

*Letter to Alexei Suvorin, Moscow, November 3, 1888*

Merezhkovsky calls my monk[13]—the one who composes hymns—a failure. How is he a failure? God grant everyone a life like his: he had faith in God, enough to eat, and the gift of composing.... Classifying people into successes and failures means looking at human nature from a narrow, biased point of view.... Are you a success or not? Am I? And what about Napoleon? And your Vasily?[14] What is the criterion here? You have to be God to tell the successes from the failures without making a mistake.... I am off to the ball.

## Drunks

*Letter to Nikolai Leykin, Moscow, December 24, 1886*

I have read the story by the new contributor Kulakov.[15] I think he can write and has gotten the kinks out of his system. However, I do not like the fact that he makes his debut with alcoholism. Tell him that describing drunks just for the sake of using some drunken expressions is a kind of cynicism. There's no easier way of breaking into writing than on the backs of drunks.

## Napoleon

*Letter to Alexei Suvorin, Moscow, October 25, 1891*

Every night I wake up and read *War and Peace*. I read with such curiosity and such naive astonishment that it is as if I had never read anything before. It is remarkably fine. Only, I do not like the passages where he writes about Napoleon. As soon as Napoleon makes an appearance, something strained creeps into the writing, along with all sorts of tricks to prove that he was much more stupid than in reality. Everything that Pierre, Prince Andrei, or even the utterly insignificant Nikolai Rostov say or do is good, intelligent, natural, and touching; everything Napoleon thinks and does is not natural, not intelligent, but inflated, and lacking in significance.

# EMOTIONS

## Cry but Without Letting the Reader Know You're Crying

*Letter to Lydia Avilova, Melikhovo, April 29, 1892*

Yes, I did write you once that one should be unemotional when writing sad stories. And you did not understand me correctly. One may weep and moan over one's stories, one may suffer right along with one's protagonists, but I suggest, one must do so in a way the reader will not notice. The more objectivity you can muster, the more powerful will be the effect you produce. This is what I meant to say.

## Knowing How to Suffer

*Letter to Dmitry Grigorovich, Moscow, January 12, 1888*

The suicide of a seventeen-year-old boy is a most intriguing and tempting topic, but one I find terrifying to tackle. Such a painful problem demands a painfully powerful response, but does "yours truly" really have the necessary inner resources to deal with it? No. When you promise success for this project, you are judging by your own resources. You overlook the fact that your generation can fall back not only on talent, but also on erudition, schooling, on "phosphorus and iron," while our generation has nothing of the sort, and, truth be told, one should rejoice that we steer clear of such serious subjects. Put your teenage suicide in their hands, and I'm sure that X, absolutely oblivious and with the most generous of intentions, will churn out a pile of slander, lies, and blasphemy; Y will throw in some vapid, pale moralizing; and Z will explain the suicide away as a psychosis. Your teenager is sweet, pure, and gentle by nature, searching for God, loving, sensitive, and hurt to the core of his being. To have a feel for this kind of person one must oneself know how to suffer, but our contemporary bards know only how to whine and snivel. As for me, I am all of the above, plus lazy and dim-witted.

## Write with Emotional Restraint

*Letter to Lydia Avilova, Moscow, March 1, 1893*

You are making great progress, but allow me to repeat my advice: write with more self-restraint. The more emotionally charged a situation, the more emotional restraint one must use in writing, and then the result will be emotionally powerful. There is no need for laying it on thick.

## Like a Strainer

*Letter to Fyodor Batyushkov, Nice, December 15, 1897*

You expressed a desire in one of your letters for me to send you an international story drawn from life in this part of the world. I can write such a story only in Russia, from memory. I can only write from memory and have never written directly from nature. I need to use my memory like a strainer so that it filters out everything that is unimportant and not specific.

## The Topic Must Be New

*Letter to Alexander Chekhov, Moscow, April 11, 1889*

Keep in mind, by the way, that professions of love, spousal infidelities, and the tears of widows, orphans, and every other species have already been described. The topic must be new, even if there is no plot.

# WHAT TO AVOID

## We Will Not Play the Quack

*Letter to Ivan Leontyev (Shcheglov), Sumy, June 9, 1888*

Apropos the ending of my "Fires," permit me to disagree with you.[16] It is not the job of the psychologist to understand what he does not understand. Moreover, it is not the job of the psychologist to pretend that he understands what no one else in fact understands. We will not play the quack; instead, we will openly declare that one cannot make sense of anything in this world. Only fools and charlatans know everything and understand everything.

## Don't Preach

*Letter to Alexei Suvorin, Moscow, April 1, 1890*

You scold me for my objectivity, calling it indifference to good and evil, lack of ideals and ideas, and so forth. When I am writing about horse thieves, you want me to say that it is evil to steal horses. However, everyone knows this already without my having to say so. Let the members of the jury pass their judgment. My job is merely to show what sort of people these horse thieves are. Here is what I write: we are dealing with horse thieves here, so bear in mind that they are not beggars but well-fed men, that they are members of a cult, and that for them stealing horses is not just thieving, but a passion. Certainly, it might be nice to combine art with preaching, but for me personally this is exceptionally difficult and technically next to impossible. After all, if I want to describe horse thieves in seven hundred lines, I have to talk and think and feel as they talk and think and feel; otherwise, if I let myself get subjective, my characters will fall apart and the story will not be as concise as all very short stories need to be. When I am writing, I rely entirely on my readers, and I trust them to fill in any subjective elements that might be missing.

## Don't Teach

*Letter to Alexei Suvorin, Melikhovo, July 28, 1893*

I did not end up writing a play based on life in Siberia and, in fact, forgot all about it, but I have gone ahead and submitted my "Sakhalin" for publication. I recommend it to your attention. Forget what you have already read of my work, because it is false. I have been writing for a long time, and I have been suspecting for a long time that I have been off course, but I have now finally figured out where I went wrong. The falseness is in my apparent desire to teach my reader something with my "Sakhalin" and, at the same time, in my hiding something and holding myself back. But as soon as I let myself describe how much of an eccentric I felt myself to be in Sakhalin and what swine those people are, then, at that point, I felt better and my work took off, even though it did turn out a touch humorous.

# Ignore the Incidental

*Letter to Alexei Suvorin, Melikhovo, April 26, 1893*
Everything time-pegged in the work—all those digs at trendy critics and liberals, all those barbs trying to be pointed and timely, and all those allegedly profound insights scattered here and there—how shallow and naive they all are with respect to our present moment! This is what it all boils down to: the novelist who wants to be an artist must ignore everything that has a merely transitory significance.

# Ornaments

*Letter to Alexei Pleshcheyev, Sumy, July 5, 1888*
I am glad for [Vladimir] Gilyarovsky. He is a good man and not without talent, though uncultivated when it comes to literature. He has a dreadful weakness for commonplaces, for bathetic words and bombastic descriptions, and thinks that without them one simply cannot write. He does have a good nose for beauty in the works of others; he knows that the first and chief excellence of a story lies in its simplicity and sincerity; but he himself is incapable of being either sincere or simple in his stories: he lacks the courage to do so. He reminds me of those believers who do not have the nerve to pray to God in their native Russian rather than in Old Church Slavonic, even though they realize that Russian lies much closer to their truth and to their hearts.

## Jargon

*Letter to Alexei Suvorin, Melikhovo, August 24, 1893*

"Nevertheless" and "insofar as" are both bureaucratic expressions. I read them and I spit. The new generation writes in an especially shabby language. Unclear, cold, and inelegant; those sons of bitches write as though they are already dead and lying in the grave.

## Don't Be Afraid to Write Nonsense

*Letter to Alexander Chekhov, Moscow, April 11, 1889*

My advice: try to be original and as clever as possible in your play, but do not be afraid of appearing stupid. Freethinking is essential, but to be a freethinker one must not be afraid to write nonsense.

## Avoid Exposés

*Letter to Ivan Leontyev (Shcheglov), Yalta, February 2, 1900*

Dear Jean, you are not the type to go in for exposés, spite, anger, so-called "independence," i.e., criticism aimed at liberals and the new generation. God gave you a kind, gentle heart, so use it and write with a gentle pen and a carefree heart and do not give a thought to the wrongs that have been done to you.... Be objective, look on everything through the eyes of a good man, through your own eyes, that is, and sit down to write a tale or a play based on Russian life, not a critique of Russian life, but a joyous hymn, the song of a goldfinch,[17] about Russian life, and indeed life in general, which is given us only once and should not be squandered on exposés of vicious wives and the Committee. Dear Jean, be fair to yourself and to your gift. Steer your ship into the open seas; do not moor it in the Fontanka.[18] Forgive everyone who has offended you, forget about them, and, I repeat, sit down and write.

# THE COMPANY OF WRITERS

## A Life of Seclusion

*Letter to Vukol Lavrov,*[19] *Moscow, April 10, 1890*

Criticism does not usually require a rebuttal, but in this instance,[20] it might be more accurate to speak not of criticism, but libel, pure and simple. Ordinarily I would not bother replying to libel, but in just a few days, I will be leaving Russia for a long time, perhaps never to return, and I lack the strength to keep from responding.

I have never been an unprincipled writer or, what amounts to the same thing, a scoundrel.

True, my entire literary career has been characterized by an unbroken string of mistakes, some of them egregious, but this can be explained by the dimensions of my talent rather than by my goodness or wickedness as a human being. I have never blackmailed anyone. I have never lampooned or libeled anyone. I have never flattered, lied, or insulted anyone. In short, though I have written many stories and editorials that I would gladly throw out as worthless, I cannot find a single line of which I should now be ashamed....

Thus far, I have led a life of seclusion, shut up within these four walls. You and I run into each other perhaps once or twice a year. I have never in my life, for instance, met Mr. Machtet.[21] You can judge from this alone how often I get out of the house. I have always steadfastly avoided literary soirées, parties, meetings, and so forth; never made an appearance in even a single editorial office without an express invitation. I have always tried to present myself to my acquaintances as a physician rather than as a man of letters: in short, I have been a modest writer, and the letter I am now writing you represents the first instance of immodesty in a career that has spanned a decade. I am on excellent terms with my colleagues. I have never taken it upon myself to judge either them or the journals and newspapers in which they publish, because I consider myself lacking the competence to do so, and because I realize that, given the present dependent position of the press, every word against a journal or a writer is not only cruel and tactless, but downright criminal. Until now I have turned down only those journals and newspapers whose inferior quality is both obvious and well proven; on those occasions when I was compelled to choose among them, I always gave priority to those that stood in the greatest need of my services either because of material or other considerations. For this reason I worked neither for your publication nor for the *European Messenger*, but for the *Northern Herald*, and as a result I have earned half as much as I would have were I to hold different views on my obligations.

## Literary Entourage

*Letter to Lydia Avilova, Melikhovo, July 23, 1898*

Suddenly I am finding writing repellent, and I do not know what to do about it. I would be glad to take up medicine and get a position somewhere, but I lack the physical agility to do this. These days, whenever I start to write or think about having to write, I feel as repelled as if I were eating cabbage soup with a cockroach floating in it—forgive the comparison. What repels me is not the writing itself, but the entire literary entourage from which you cannot hide and which you carry around yourself everywhere you go, the way the Earth carries around its atmosphere.

## Academy of Sciences

*Letter to the Academy of Sciences, 1902*[22]

Your Imperial Highness!

In December of last year, I received notification that A. M. Peshkov[23] was elected to the position of Honorary Member of the Academy of Sciences. I wasted no time in seeing A. M. Peshkov, who was at that time sojourning in the Crimea: I was the first to bring him news of his election, and I was the first to offer him my congratulations. Shortly thereafter, the press reported that in view of the charges brought against Peshkov under Paragraph 1035, the election results were pronounced null and void. Moreover, it was clearly indicated that this pronouncement proceeded from the Academy of Sciences, and inasmuch as I am myself an Honorary Member of the Academy, it follows that this pronouncement proceeded from me as well. I offered my heartfelt congratulations and at the same time, I declared the election results to be null and void: it was impossible for me to resolve this contradiction in my own mind or to reconcile it with my conscience. Acquainting myself with the provisions of Paragraph 1035, I failed to arrive at any clarification. And after having given the matter much serious and deep deliberation, I was able to arrive at the decision, a very difficult and painful decision, that I must most respectfully beg Your Imperial Highness to divest me of my honorary membership in the Academy.

## Intelligentsia

*Letter to Ivan Orlov,*[24] *Yalta, February 22, 1899*

I have no faith in our intelligentsia, for it is hypocritical, dishonest, hysterical, uncultured, and lazy. I have no faith in it even when it claims to be suffering and is protesting, for its oppressors issue from its very own loins. I do have faith in individuals. I see salvation in individuals—intellectuals and peasants alike—scattered here and there across Russia, for though they may be few, they have real strength. A prophet has no honor in his own land, and the individuals of whom I speak play an almost imperceptible role in our society. Though they do not dominate, their deeds are manifest. No matter what you might say or do, science is constantly moving forward, social awareness is growing, moral issues are becoming increasingly alarming, etc. etc. And all this takes place irrespective of procurators, engineers, and governors, irrespective of the intelligentsia *en masse*, and in spite of everything.

## Sparrows on a Pile of Manure

*Undated letter [1900?]*[25]

I will be reproved for writing only about mediocre events, for not having any positive heroes....

We are leading a provincial life, the streets of our city are not even paved, our villages are poor, and our people are worn out. In our youth, we twitter like a bunch of sparrows on a pile of manure. At forty we are already old and starting to think about death. What sort of heroes are we?...

I only wanted to tell people honestly: look, look how badly you live, how boring your lives are. The important thing is that people should understand this; if they do understand this, they will certainly invent a different and a far better life. Man will become better only once we have shown him as he really is.

## Keep Away from Politics

*Letter to Alexei Suvorin, Nice, February 6, 1898*

Bit by bit, people came to be persuaded that Dreyfus had in fact been condemned on the basis of a secret document that had not been shown either to the defendant or his attorney.[26]

...I am familiar with the trial from the stenographic record, which is totally different from the newspaper reports, and I have a clear understanding of Zola. The main thing here is that he is sincere, that is, he bases his judgments only on what he can actually see, and not, like others, on phantoms. Of course, even sincere people can make mistakes, but their mistakes cause less harm than premeditated insincerity, prejudice, or political motives. Suppose Dreyfus is guilty: Zola is still right because it is not the writer's job to accuse and to prosecute, but to rise to the defense even of the guilty once they have been condemned and are being punished. People will object, "What about politics? What about the interests of the state?" But great writers and artists should take an interest in politics only to the degree that is necessary for them to protect themselves. Even without them, there are enough accusers, prosecutors, and secret police to go around.

## New and Old Talent on the Editorial Board

*Letter to Nikolai Leykin, Moscow, September 2, 1887*

The debut of fresh energies should be fully supported and indulged: this has been my long-standing position, and I want to reiterate it in the present instance.... The editorial board, in my view, should utilize fresh talent by first putting them to work on minor assignments. As far as I recall, Èber started out the normal way, i.e., small, and Chemodan began by drawing pictures for the rebus section.[27]...

As far as redoing the editorial board, revitalizing it, and so on, we have already discussed this in person and in writing. You write that we, the old contributors, keep chewing the same old cud. No, we have stayed exactly the same because we are incapable of changing our literary physiognomies; this is why it only seems we keep chewing the same old cud. We write too much and too often and so have managed to exhaust not our reading public, which keeps changing, but our selves; in another five years we will be totally repulsive, but just to ourselves. I happen to think that an influx of new energies would benefit the public little, but would benefit us a lot: we would gain the right to write as we feel like writing, and that would look a lot more like art than the present piecework we turn out, and we would be much happier with ourselves than we are now.

## Refuse Censoring

*Letter to Alexei Suvorin, Yalta, March 4, 1899*

Here as everywhere else, there is much talk about the student disturbances and a great deal of outcry about the lack of coverage in the papers.[28] Letters from St. Petersburg indicate that public sentiment is on the side of the students. Your columns on the disturbances failed to satisfy, but this could not be otherwise because it is impossible to pass judgment on the disorders in print when all mention of the facts is forbidden. The state forbade you to write, it forbids speaking the truth: this is arbitrary rule, and yet you write lightheartedly about the rights and prerogatives of the state in connection with this arbitrary rule. The mind simply cannot make sense of all this. You speak about the right of the state, but you are not viewing the matter from a legal point of view. When it comes to the state, rights and justice are identical to those of any juridical person. If the state unjustly alienates a piece of my land, I can sue it in court, and the court will restore to me what is mine by right. Should not the same be the case when the state takes up the knout to beat me? If it aggresses against me, should I not be able to protest a violation of my rights? The concept of the state should be founded on precise legal relations. If it is not, the state is a bogeyman, a hollow noise producing an imaginary fright.

# PART TWO: DEMONSTRATION

## Good Shoes and a Notebook

# 3

# THE PROJECT

❦

## A Change of Air

*Travel to overcome inertia and do not expect to write.*

Letter to Alexei Suvorin, March 9, 1890

I imagine the journey will be six months of constant physical and mental work, which is precisely what my sluggish nature requires. I need self-discipline. Granted, this journey might be nothing more than a frivolous, headstrong caprice, but tell me, what do I stand to lose? Time? Money? And what do I stand to gain—a lot of hardship? My time is worth nothing. I have no money to speak of. And as for hardship, I'll have twenty-five—maybe thirty—days on horseback, and the rest of the time I'll be sitting on the deck of a steamer or in my room writing letters to you. Even if I get nothing out of the journey, I cannot imagine not coming away without two or three days that will remain as joyous or bitter memories to the very end of my life.

## Pay No Attention to Critics

*No response to critics is needed. Listen to your own conscience.*

*Letter to Ivan Leontyev (Shcheglov), March 22, 1890*

You write that you want to give me a sound scolding, "especially on ethical and aesthetic matters"; you say something vague about certain sins of mine that call for a friendly rebuke, and even threaten me with "influential newspaper critics." Is it possible that my ethics are out of line with the views of good people such as yourself, and to such an extent that I deserve to be scolded and brought to the attention of influential critics?…If my clear conscience can be trusted, I have never in word, deed, thought, in stories or in farces: coveted my neighbor's wife or servant or oxen or cattle; I have not stolen, played the hypocrite, flattered or toadied to the mighty; I have not blackmailed anyone or lived at anyone's expense. True: I have wasted my life in idleness; I have laughed without provocation; I have indulged in gluttony and defiled myself with drunkenness; I have dissipated myself in fornication. However, all this is my personal business and does not take away my right to consider myself neither more nor less moral than the common run of humanity….

If those critics whose authority you cite know something that you and I do not, then, tell me, why haven't they spoken up all this time and revealed their truths and immutable laws to us? Believe me, if they had actually known something along this line, they would most certainly have pointed us in the right direction long ago, and you and I would have known what to do…. You and I would not have been as bored as we are now, and you wouldn't have been drawn to the theater nor I to Sakhalin.... But the critics maintain a dignified silence or carry on with their idle blather. If you find them influential, that is only because they are stupid, pretentious, aggressive, and strident: empty barrels rattling in your ears.

To hell with all that. Let us move on to another subject. Please do not expect anything artistic to come out of my Sakhalin journey. I am not going for observations or impressions, but only to spend six months living in a way I have not lived yet up to now. Do not place any great hopes in me, my friend. If I do manage to accomplish something, praise the Lord; if not, do not blame me. I will be leaving the week after Easter.

## Talk Things Over with Friends

*Clarify the areas and scope of your research in discussions with friends.*

*Letter to Alexei Suvorin, March 9, 1890*

We are both wrong about Sakhalin, but probably you more so than I. I am going there certain that my trip will contribute nothing of value either to art or to science. I lack the knowledge, time, and ambition for that. I have no plans on the scale of Humboldt's or Kennan's.[1] I intend to write between 100 and 200 pages so I can pay off some of my debt to medicine, in regard to which I have been a perfect swine....

Sakhalin is a place of such unbearable suffering as only man, free or captive, is capable of inflicting. Those working on and around it have been trying to find solutions to horrendous, weighty problems. I regret I am not sentimental or I would say that we should be bound to make pilgrimages to places such as Sakhalin the way Turks go to Mecca, and that sailors and experts on penal servitude should regard Sakhalin in the same way the military regards Sebastopol.[2] The books I have read and am currently reading make it clear that we have condemned *millions* of human beings to rot in prisons; we have condemned them barbarically, for no purpose at all, without thinking; we have herded human beings tens of thousands of miles across the cold, in chains; we have infected them with syphilis, debauched them, multiplied the number of criminals, and we have put all the blame for this on the red-nosed prison wardens. Nowadays all educated Europeans know that prison wardens are not to blame, but we go on insisting that this is none of our business and cannot interest us. The vaunted sixties[3] did absolutely *nothing* for the sick and the imprisoned and thereby violated the central commandment of Christian civilization. Our age is doing something for the sick, but nothing for the imprisoned; our legal experts have absolutely no interest in penology. No, I assure you, Sakhalin is necessary and interesting; the only regrettable thing is that I am going there—rather than someone with more expertise and more ability to arouse public opinion. After all, I am traveling there on a trivial pretext.

## Challenge Indifference

*Study those areas that no one else studies; go in person to see the injustices that no one else sees; value firsthand experience and hands-on knowledge.*

Anton Chekhov, *"From Siberia,"* The Island of Sakhalin
*(travel notes), May 18, 1890*

I am deeply convinced that in fifty or a hundred years' time people will look upon our sentences of life imprisonment with the same dismay and distress with which we now view the slitting of nostrils and the amputation of fingers from the left hand. I am equally convinced that though we may sincerely and clearly acknowledge that such archaic phenomena as life imprisonment are obsolete and pernicious, we are utterly impotent to stop them. At present, we lack the knowledge, experience, and, perhaps, courage to replace the life sentence with something more rational and just. All our attempts to do so are indecisive and tentative and consequently can produce only grave errors and extremes: this is the fate of all undertakings not grounded in knowledge and experience....

For the past twenty or thirty years our thinking intellectuals have been repeating the phrase that criminals are produced by society, and yet how indifferent they are to this product! The cause for this indifference—quite incomprehensible in a Christian state and a Christian literature—to prisoners and exiles lies in the abysmally shallow education of our Russian lawyer. He knows little. He is encumbered with professional biases.... He takes his university examinations so he can learn how to go about judging and sentencing others to jail or to exile. However, he himself has no idea what happens to the criminal after trial, and why, and what prison and Siberia might be like, and all this is beyond his sphere of interests or his area of expertise. All this is a matter for the convoys and the prison wardens with their red noses!

## Read and Summarize

*Do research and take notes; ask for help and borrow books; read everything except what fails to give facts.*

*Letter to Alexei Pleshcheyev, February 15, 1890*

I have been sitting here all day long, reading, and taking notes. There is nothing in my head or on paper except Sakhalin. Mental derangement. *Mania Sakhalinosa.*[4]

*Letter to Alexei Suvorin, February 23, 1890*

If you happen to come across Tsebrikova's article, do not bother sending it to me.[5] Articles like hers do not give any real information and are a waste of time. I need facts. In general, there is a dreadful dearth of facts and a dreadful wealth of speculation in our Rus,[6] as I am coming to realize through my zealous study of literature on Sakhalin.

*Letter to Modest Tchaikovsky, March 16, 1890*

I am shut up at home, sitting and reading about the price of a ton of coal on Sakhalin and in Shanghai in 1883. I am reading about the force of winds from the northeast, northwest, southeast, and other directions that will be blowing on me as

I will be observing the symptoms of my own seasickness on the shores of Sakhalin. I am reading about the soil, the sub-soil, the sandy loam, and the loamy sand.

*Letter to Alexei Suvorin, March 22, 1890*

Do you happen to have in your library Voycykov's *Climates of Various Lands?*[7] It is an excellent work. If you do have it, please send it; if not, do not bother because it costs five rubles, which is a lot of money for me. Send me Maksimov's *Siberia and Penal Servitude.*[8]

## Write Up the Notes

*Write the parts that do not rely on field research, using the material from your readings, notes, and summaries; consult maps to describe how perceptions of an area have changed over time.*

*Letter to Alexei Suvorin, March 22, 1890*

I have already started writing about Sakhalin. I have about five pages on the history of exploration. They have turned out quite well, perhaps even intelligent and authoritative. I have also made a stab at the geography, the degrees and latitudes and promontories.

In June 1787, the renowned French navigator Count de La Pérouse landed on the western shore of Sakhalin, above the 48th parallel, and came into contact with the indigenous people. There, by his account, he found the Ainu had settled on the seashore, as well as the Ghiliak who had come to trade, and who had an excellent knowledge of Sakhalin and the Tartar coast. Drawing on the sand, they explained to him that the land they had settled was an island and that this island was separated from the continent and from Yezo (Japan) by several straits.... He expected that by sailing further north along the western shore, he would find a passage from the Sea of Japan into the Sea of Okhotsk, thereby significantly cutting the time it took to reach Kamchatka. As he progressed farther north, however, the strait became increasingly shallow, the depth decreasing by about seven feet per mile of distance. He continued north as long as his vessel permitted and, advancing to a depth of about eight fathoms, cast anchor. The gradual and regular rise in the level of the seafloor as well as the nearly imperceptible current suggested that they had entered a bay rather than a strait, and that an isthmus connected Sakhalin to the mainland. In De Castries, he again came into contact with the Ghiliaks. As he was making them a drawing to show how the island was detached from the mainland, one of the Ghiliaks took his pencil out of his hand and, tracing a line across the strait, indicated that the Ghiliaks occasionally dragged their boats across the isthmus, which, moreover, was sometimes even covered with grass, as La Pérouse understood them to be saying. This convinced the navigator even more firmly that Sakhalin was a peninsula.[9]

In 1710, under order of the Chinese emperor, missionaries from Beijing produced a map of Tartaria that could only have been based on Japanese maps, since at the time only the Japanese knew the Tartar straits to be navigable. This information was relayed to France and was disseminated through the atlas of the geographer D'Anville.[10]

# 4

# THE REPORT

The mind of a scientist is always placed, as it were,
between two observations: one which serves as a
starting point for reasoning, and the other which
serves as conclusion.

—CLAUDE BERNARD
*Introduction to the Study of Experimental Medicine (1865)*

## PREREQUISITES

### Good Shoes

*Do not scrimp on boots.*

*Letter to Maria Chekhova, May 14–17, 1890*

I think going barefoot must be better than wearing cheap
boots. You cannot imagine my suffering! Now and then, I
crawl out of my carriage, get down on the wet ground, and
pull off my boots to give my heels a break. A rare pleasure in
the freezing cold! I ended up buying felt boots[1] in Ishim…and

wore them until they fell apart from the damp and the mud....

We set off.... Mud, rain, a piercing cold wind...and felt boots on my feet. Do you know what felt boots are like when they are wet? Gelatin. We drive along and suddenly right in front of my eyes there is a huge lake with a few patches of land and some bushes sticking out here and there—and this turns out to be flooded grasslands. Across the far horizon stretches the steep bank of the Irtys River; it's white with snow.... We start across the lake. We ought really turn back, but one of those fits of obstinacy comes over me, just like the time in the middle of the Black Sea when I dove off the yacht and all those other times when my stubborn streak made me do all sorts of stupid things....

At last, we reach a tiny island on which there is a little hut without a roof.... There are wet horses shuffling in the wet manure. A peasant comes out of the hut with a long pole in his hand and offers to show us the way.... He uses the pole to sound the depth of the water and test the footing.... God grant him health....

We continue on our way.... My boots are wetter than a toilet and make a snuffling sound, like socks blowing their noses.

# Notebook

*Always keep a notebook on hand to jot down facts, observations, turns of phrase, and to record statements and interviews.*

The prison is badly ventilated, and there is little air for each inmate. My diary entry reads: "Barrack No. 9. Volume of air—1,309 cubic feet. There are 65 inmates." And this in the summer, when only half the inmates spend the night indoors.[2]

[A compulsive card player] told me that when he is playing *shtoss*[3] he feels "electricity in his veins"; the tension cramps his hands. He loves to reminisce about how as a young man he won a watch from the chief of police. Talking about shtoss fills him with rapture. I remember he pronounced the word "Missed!" with the despair of a hunter whose gun misfired. I have noted down some of his expressions for the benefit of amateurs: "Transport's done! Ready! Arm! A ruble a point! Aim! Color and suit! Artillery: fire!"

When I appeared before the Governor General with paper in hand, he proceeded to outline for me his views on the Sakhalin penal system and colony and proposed I take down everything he said, which I, of course, most readily agreed to do. He suggested I give the following title to the notes: "A Description of the Life of the Unfortunates." Everything he said in our last conversation and what he dictated to me persuaded me that while he might have been a magnanimous and noble human being, he knew less about the "life of the unfortunates" than he gave himself credit for knowing. Here, for example, are some examples of his observations: "No one is deprived of the hope of becoming fully enfranchised; there is no life imprisonment. An indefinite sentence is limited to twenty years. Penal labor is not oppressive. It is not because it is physically difficult, but because it gives the worker no personal gain that involuntary labor is oppressive. There are no chains, no guards, no shaved heads."

## Be Ready to Revise Your Opinions

*Be ready to revise opinions based on readings and expectations.*

I had read a great deal about the gales and the ice floes in the Tatar Strait, and so on board the *Baikal* I expected to meet hoarse whalers spitting tobacco juice with every word. In fact, the people I met were quite cultivated. Mr. L, the ship's captain, a native of a western country, had been sailing in the northern seas for over thirty years and had crossed them from end to end. He has seen many marvelous things in his time, knows a great deal, and has a most interesting way of telling stories. After half a lifetime of sailing around Kamchatka and the Kurile Islands, he can compete with Othello in speaking of "Tempests themselves, high seas, and howling winds, / The gutter'd rocks and congregated sands."[4] I owe him a considerable debt for much of the information contained in these notes. He had three assistants: a Mr. B, nephew of the famous astronomer B, and the Swedes Ivan Martynich and Ivan Veniaminych, both fine and affable men.

# TRAVEL

## Do Not Get Discouraged

*Do not be put off by initial difficulties and fear of the unforeseen.*

However, back to my story. As it was getting late in the day and I had not been able to find lodgings on shore, I decided to board the *Baikal.* But here too I met with a setback: the sea had turned rough and the Ghiliak boatmen refused to row me across at any price. I was back to walking up and down the shore wondering what to do. The sun was going down and the waves turned black on the Amur. From both banks rose the frenzied howling of Ghiliak dogs. "Now what exactly was my reason for coming here?" I asked myself, beginning to suspect that it had been sheer folly to undertake this trip. The realization that the convict colony was now quite near, that in a matter of days I would disembark on Sakhalin without even an official letter of introduction, that I could be told to turn back—this realization gnawed at me most disagreeably. At last, however, two Ghiliaks consented to row me over for a ruble, and I reached the *Baikal* unharmed in a rowboat knocked together out of three boards.

...[It] was calm and clear, which is rare in these waters. On the smooth surface of the sea, pairs of whales blew jets of water high into the air and this beautiful, original spectacle kept us entertained during the entire crossing. I have to admit, however, that my spirits were low and sank even lower as we drew close to Sakhalin. I was uneasy. The officer accompanying the soldiers was amazed to learn my reason for going to Sakhalin and insisted that lacking an official position, I had absolutely no right to visit the penal colony. I knew he was wrong, of course, but his words depressed me all the same, and I worried that I would meet with the same views on Sakhalin.

...I spent the night on board. Early the next morning, at about five, loud shouts woke me. "Hurry! Hurry! Last run to shore! The cutter's leaving!" In an instant, I boarded the cutter, and took my place next to a young official with an angry, sleepy face. The whistle sounded, and we made for the shore, towing two barges full of convicts. The prisoners were sluggish and gloomy, exhausted by their night's labor and lack of sleep; no one spoke. Their faces were covered with dew. I remember several sharp-featured Caucasians with fur hats pulled low over their brows.

...Everything that yesterday had seemed so dark and menacing and threatened the worst was now melting in the early morning brilliance. Fat, clunky Cape Zhonkier with its lighthouse, the "Three Brothers,"[5] the high, craggy coastline visible on both sides from a distance of several dozen miles, the transparent mist on the mountains, and the smoke from the fires—nothing looked terrifying in the brilliant sunlight.

## Do Not Make Too Many Plans

*Sometimes it is useful to leave things up to chance, especially when in an unfamiliar setting.*

On shore, someone's horse was standing harnessed to a buggy without springs. Convicts put my bags on the buggy; a man with a black beard wearing a jacket over long shirttails climbed up on the box. We started.

"Where to, your worship?" he asked, turning around and doffing his cap.

I asked whether he knew of an apartment or even a room for rent.

"Certainly, your worship, there is something for rent."

...The driver took me to the Aleksadrovskaya Slobodka, a district in the suburbs, to the house of P, one of the peasant exiles. I was shown my lodgings.

After services on September 8, a holy day,[6] I was just leaving the church in the company of a young official when a corpse was brought in on a stretcher. The pallbearers—four ragged convicts with coarse faces ravaged by alcohol—looked just like the beggars in our cities. They were followed by two more, just like them, who made up the reserve, and also a woman with two children, and a dark Georgian, Kelbokiani, dressed in the attire of a free man (he works as a scribe and is called "Prince"), and all of them seemed to be in a hurry, afraid of missing the priest. Kelbokiani told us that the deceased was a free woman named Lyalikova whose husband, a settler, had gone to Nikolayevsk. The two children were hers,

and now he, Kelbokiani, her lodger, had no idea what he was
to do with them. Having no better alternatives, my companion and I went ahead to the cemetery without waiting for the
end of the funeral service.

## Accept Invitations

*Go to dinner, pay attention to the furnishings and the food, lis-
ten to the guests, and take part in the conversation.*

While I was talking with the clerk, into the shop walked the
owner,[7] dressed in a silk jacket and flashy tie. We introduced
ourselves.

"Won't you be so kind as to have dinner at my home?" he
proposed.

I agreed, and off we went. He lived comfortably: furniture from Vienna, flowers, an American Aristone gramo-
phone, and a bentwood rocker on which L sits after dinner.
In addition to the housewife, the dining room held four
guests, all officials. One, an old man without a mustache
and with gray sideburns that made him look like the playwright Ibsen, turned out to be the junior physician at the
local infirmary. Another, also old, introduced himself as a
staff officer of the Orienburg Cossack Army. From his very
first words, this officer impressed me as a very kindly individual and a great patriot. He was meek and good-natured
in his judgments, but when he started to discuss politics, he
came out of his shell and spoke with passion about the
power of Russia's military and with scorn about the Ger-

mans and the British, of whom he had absolutely no personal experience. Once, when traveling to Sakhalin, he had wanted to buy his wife a silk shawl in Singapore. When told he would have to change Russian money into dollars, he took great offense and said, "What next! Exchange my Orthodox money for some kind of Ethiopian money?!" And the shawl was not bought.

Dinner consisted of soup, chicken, and ice cream. Wine was also served.

"When, roughly, do you have your last snowfall here?" I asked.

"In May," L answered.

"Wrong. In June," snapped the doctor who looked like Ibsen.

"I know a settler," said L, "whose California wheat yielded twenty-two-fold. I know him personally."

Another objection from the doctor.

"Wrong. Your Sakhalin yields exactly zero. It's an accursed land."

"Nevertheless, if you please," said one of the officials, "in '82 the wheat yielded forty-fold. I know this for a fact."

"Don't you believe him," the doctor warned me. "They're just pulling wool over your eyes."

At dinner the following legend was told: when the Russians took possession of the island and set about harassing the Ghiliaks, the Ghiliak shaman laid a curse on Sakhalin and predicted that nothing good would ever come of it.

"And that's precisely what happened," sighed the doctor.

## Take Walks

*Take walks with a companion or by yourself, to talk things over and try to get a detached view of things.*

I have pleasant memories of walks around Aleksandrovsk and the area with the postmaster, the author of *Sakhalinó.*[8] Our favorite destination was the lighthouse situated high above the valley on Cape Zhonkier. When you look up at it by daylight, you see a modest little house with a mast and a lantern, but at night, when it shines brilliantly in the dark, penal servitude itself seems to be staring out through its red eye. The road to the lighthouse climbs steeply, spiraling around the mountain past ancient larches and firs. The higher you climb, the freer you breathe. The sea stretches out before you. Slowly your mind fills with thoughts that have nothing to do with prison, penal servitude, and the exile colony, and you begin to appreciate the tedium and duress of the life below. Day in and day out the convicts and exiles endure their punishment, while from morning to night the free people talk of nothing but who got a flogging, and who tried to escape, and who was caught, and who would get a flogging. And, strange to say, after only a single week you find yourself getting used to these conversations and interests and the first thing you do when you wake up in the morning is rush to read the general orders—the local daily paper—and then all day long you listen and talk about who tried to escape, and who was shot down, etc. On the mountain, however, looking out toward the sea and the beautiful ravines, you suddenly find all this talk utterly banal and vulgar, as, indeed, it is.

## Keep Your Eyes Open

*On the road, pay attention to everything.*

I traveled the two versts[9] between the harbor and the Aleksandrovsk Post on a superlative road. In comparison with Siberian roads, this clean, smooth highway—with ditches and lampposts—is an utter luxury. Alongside it runs the railway. The natural landscape, however, is striking in its bareness. The mountaintops and hills flanking Aleksandrovsk Valley through which the Duyka River flows bristle with charred stumps and larches killed by the wind and the fires that project like porcupine quills, while down below, in the valley, hummocks and sorrel are all that remains of the once impassable swamps. The freshly dug ditches expose muddy, scorched soil with a paltry half-inch of *chernozem*[10] still clinging to it. Not a spruce, oak, or maple in sight: there are only larches—emaciated, pitiful, and gnawed-looking—those same larches that in Russia ornament woodlands and parks, and here signal the presence of poor, marshy soil and a harsh climate. The Aleksandrovsk Post, or Aleksandrovsk for short, is a small, attractive town of the Siberian type, with a population of some three thousand. It has no stone structures; everything—the church, houses, and sidewalks—is made of wood, mainly larch. Here is the island commandant's residence, the very center of Sakhalin civilization. The prison is situated close to the main street; from the outside, it resembles an army barracks, which is chiefly why Aleksandrovsk lacks that gloomy prison atmosphere that I expected to find here.

## Go on Excursions

*Travel by foot, in company, and make detours.*

On August 27, General Kononovich arrived. He was accompanied by the director of the Tymovsk district and another official, a young man. All three were intelligent and interesting people. The four of us ventured on a short excursion, which, however, entailed so much discomfort that it felt more like a parody of an expedition than an actual excursion. To begin with, it was pouring rain. The footing was muddy, slippery; everything one touched was wet. Water seeped inside our collars and down our backs. Our boots were cold and wet. Lighting a cigarette turned out to be a complicated, difficult undertaking that required the combined efforts of the entire group. We got into a boat near Debrinskoye and set off down the Tym River.... The current ran swift. The four rowers and the steersman worked in harmony. Thanks to the speed and the frequent bends in the river, the scenery changed every minute. We were carried along on a mountain taiga river, but I would gladly have exchanged its wild charms, green banks, steep hills, and the motionless forms of the fishermen for a warm room and a pair of dry boots, especially since the scenery ended up being monotonous and offered me nothing novel, and, to make matters worse, was shrouded in a gray, rainy mist. A. M. Butakov sat in front with his rifle and kept taking shots at the wild ducks that we startled by our passage.

...Shortly after this, there came a ferocious stench of rotting fish. We were approaching the Ghiliak village Usk-vo, now called Uskovo. On the bank we were met by Ghiliak men, their wives, children, and dock-tailed dogs, none of them showing the sort of amazement that the late Polyakov's arrival had produced. Even the dogs and the children looked at us with complete indifference.

...After a rest, at about five in the afternoon, we set off to walk back to Voskresenskoye. The distance was insignificant, some six versts in all, but because of my inexperience with walking in the taiga, I was fatigued after only the first mile. A heavy rain kept falling. Right after leaving Uskov we had to negotiate a stream about ten feet wide spanned by three narrow, crooked logs; everyone managed to cross, but I slipped and water got into my boot. Ahead of us, through the forest, lay a long, straight cut for the future road. It was impossible to make one's way without losing one's balance or stumbling: hillocks, holes full of water, bushes as stiff as wire, roots lurking under the water to trip one up like a doorstep, and—worst and most annoying of all—the windthrow and the piles of logs that had been cut down for the road. You conquer one heap, drenched with sweat, and slog on through the swamp, and then another pile looms up ahead of you, and there's no getting around this one and as you're hauling yourself up the side your companions start shouting that you're going the wrong way, you should take a left or a right around the pile, etc. At first, I tried to focus on keeping my other boot dry, but then decided to give it up and resigned myself to whatever chance might throw my way. I could hear the labored breathing of the three colonists struggling to keep up with us as they hauled our belongings. The suffocating

weather, the shortness of breath, the thirst were oppressive....
We took off our caps to make the going easier.

Wheezing, the general lowered himself on a large log. We
sat down beside him. We offered each of the colonists a cigarette, but they did not dare sit.

"Phew! It's hard going!"

"How many miles to Voskresenskoye?"

"Two maybe."

...Halfway there, we noticed the light was starting to fade
and soon we were in total darkness. I despaired of seeing the
end of the excursion and made my way by feel, blundering
through knee-high water and stumbling over logs. Here and
there, will-o'-the-wisps flickered and glimmered around my
companions and me; pools of water and huge rotting trees
glowed with phosphorescent light, and my boots sparkled
with moving specks that shone like fireflies.

At last, praise God, a light—not phosphorescence, but an
actual light—appeared far ahead of us. Someone shouted,
we shouted back; the warden came into view carrying a
lantern. He took big strides across the pools, the water re-
flecting his lantern, and guided us to his warden's hut across
the whole of Voskresenskoye, now barely visible in the
dark.[11] My companions had brought a change of clothing,
which they put on as soon as we reached the warden's hut. I,
however, though literally soaked to the bone, had nothing
dry. We filled up on tea, chatted, and then bedded down for
the night. There was only one bed in the hut and the general
took it, while we mere mortals stretched out on the hay that
was piled up on the floor.

## Get Help

*Get help, especially when you lack the power or the resources for doing something on your own.*

I was tired or maybe just lazy and was not working as hard in the south as I had been in the north. I often spent whole days hiking and going on picnics, and no longer felt like visiting huts, so whenever anyone kindly offered help, I did not refuse it. I made my first trip to the Okhotsk Sea in the company of a Mr. Bely, who wanted to show me his region. Later, when conducting my census, I always had the company of the settlement inspector N. N. Yartsev.

The doors of all the buildings [of the Aleksandrovsk prison] are left wide open. I walk through one set into a short corridor. Doors to the right and left open into the prison wards. Above the doors hang black signs with white lettering: Cell number: XYZ. Cubic volume of air: X. Number of prisoners: X. At the very end of the corridor, a door opens into a tiny cell. Two political prisoners in unbuttoned waistcoats, their feet bare in their shoes, rush to plump up their straw-filled mattress. A pamphlet and a piece of black bread lie on the windowsill. My guide, the district commander, explains that these two prisoners were given permission to live outside the prison, but did not wish to distinguish themselves from the rest of the convicts and choose not to take advantage of this permission.

## Do Practical Things

*Do something to pass the time or, if the occasion presents itself, do some useful work. This may help you with your observations.*

The *Baikal* having to unload seventy-two tons of government cargo, we stayed the night in De Castries. The machinist and I passed the time fishing off the deck and caught some huge fat-headed gobies, the likes of which I had never caught in the Black Sea or the Sea of Azov. We caught some plaice as well.

Unloading cargo is an excruciatingly long proposition here, accomplished with much ill will and bad blood.... From the deck of the *Baikal*, I watch a tugboat towing a large barge with two hundred soldiers on board and see it lose the towline. The barge slips away on the outgoing tide and heads straight for the anchor chain of a steamship moored near our ship. With sinking hearts, we wait for the moment when the barge will break in half against the chain, but fortunately, some good men catch the line just in time and the soldiers get off with nothing more than a bad fright.

A little later, I see to the ambulatory patients. The receiving room is next to the pharmacy and smells of fresh wood and varnish. The physician's desk stands in the kind of wooden cage that one sees in banks. This ensures that during the medical exam the patient never comes too close to the physician. A medic sits next to the physician silently fiddling with a pencil stub, as if he were the one being examined.

At the entrance to the room, an armed guard stands by the door keeping watch over the men and women who are milling about. This bizarre arrangement is upsetting to the patients: I doubt the syphilitics or the women would wish to discuss their symptoms in the presence of the gun-toting guard and the other men. Their ailments are either *febris sachaliensis*,[12] or eczema, or their "heart hurts," or they are malingerers. Convict patients obstinately clamor to be released from labor.

A young boy comes in with an abscess on his neck that requires lancing. I ask for a scalpel. The medic and two men leap up and run off; after a while they come back and hand me a scalpel. The instrument is dull, but they insist that this is not possible because the blacksmith has just sharpened it. Again, the medic and the men run off and after some two or three minutes they are back with a fresh scalpel. I start to make an incision, but the blade on this one too is dull. I ask for some carbolic acid in solution. They bring it, but only after making me wait for a long time. It is obvious that the disinfectant is rarely used. There is no basin, no cotton swabs, no probes, and no decent scissors; there is not even enough water.

## Join Celebrations

*Observe the preparations, rites, and participants; note the atmosphere.*

Sakhalin was getting ready for the upcoming visit of the Governor-General, and everyone was busy.... When I awoke in the morning, a very particular blend of sounds reminded me of where I was. Outside my open windows, convicts walked along with the measured clanging of chains; across the street from our quarters, in the military barracks, musician-soldiers were running through the marches selected to welcome the Governor-General. The flautist was practicing one passage, the trombonist another, the bassoon a third, and the result was a chaos beyond imagining.... Workers were rushing to construct a bridge over the Duyka. Everyone was cleaning, painting, sweeping, and marching. The streets bustled with troikas and teams of horses with bells on their harness; other horses were being curried and brushed for the Governor-General. Time was short, so the work had to continue right through the holidays.

...Baron A. N. Korf, the Governor-General of the Amur region, arrived on Sakhalin on July 19 on the warship *Bobr*. The official welcome was given by an honor guard, officials, and an assembly of exiles and convicts, and was held on the square between the commandant's residence and the church. The music described above was performed. The bread and salt were displayed on a silver platter of local workmanship and were presented by a striking old man, Potemkin by name, who had once been a convict but was now a wealthy resident of Sakhalin.[13] My host, the physician, was also in the square, dressed in a black frock coat and a cap and holding a petition.

This was the first time I had seen a crowd on Sakhalin and I was struck by its uniquely sad character: it was composed of men and women of working age, of old men and children, but there were absolutely no adolescents. It seemed as if the years from thirteen through twenty simply did not exist on Sakhalin. I could not resist asking myself, "Does this mean that as soon as they're old enough, youngsters escape from the island the first chance they get?"

The day after his arrival, the Governor-General undertook to inspect the prisons and the exile settlements. Everywhere he went, exiles who had waited impatiently for his visit pressed their written petitions on him or made their verbal appeals. Some spoke on their own behalf, others in the name of an entire village, and since oratory is a flourishing art form on Sakhalin, there was quite a great number of these speeches. In Derbinsk, the settler Maslov several times referred to the authorities as "our very most clement governors." Unfortunately, only a fraction of the appeals to Baron A. N. Korf were sensible. As happened on similar occasions in other parts of Russia, here too our peasantry's disappointing ignorance came to the fore: they did not ask for schools, justice, or fair wages. Instead, they wanted the most incidental of concessions: bigger rations, the right to adopt a particular child, etc. In other words, they submitted petitions that the local authorities could have granted locally. Nevertheless, A. N. Korf was attentive and sympathetic to their requests. Evidently deeply moved by their wretched circumstances, he made promises and raised hopes for improvement.[14] After the assistant supervisor of the Arkovo prison reported that "all is well in the Arkovo settlement," the Baron drew his attention to the winter and spring grain yields and said, "All is well, except that there is no grain in Arkovo." The inmates of Aleksandrovsk prison received fresh meat and even venison in honor of his visit. He made the rounds of all the cells, listened to the petitions, and ordered the chains removed from many of the prisoners.

...In the evening, there were fireworks and illuminations. Late into the night groups of soldiers, exiles, and convicts milled about the streets illuminated with oil lamps and Bengal lights. The prison gates stood wide open. The Duyka River, whose bare banks ordinarily made it look miserable and filthy, now appeared beautiful and even majestic in the glow of colorful lanterns and Bengal lights whose reflections flickered on the surface of the water. There was, however, something ludicrous about the entire effect, as if a cook's daughter had been made to wear her mistress's gown. There was music and singing in the general's garden. There was even an attempt to fire the cannon, but it ended in an explosion. Yet, despite all these amusements, the streets were dreary. No singing, no accordion playing, not even a drunk: people moved like ghosts in a ghostly silence. Penal servitude by the light of fancy illuminations is still penal servitude, and the distant music heard by a man forever exiled from his native land can do no more than bring on deadly melancholy.

## Go to a Wedding

*Observe what people are wearing, their ages, rituals, conversations, and social roles; try to figure out what they are feeling.*

One evening in Aleksandrovsk the local priest, Father Yegor, dropped by for a brief visit before going to church to officiate at a wedding. I came along. In the church, candles were just being lit; the singers had already assembled in the choir loft and were waiting for the bridal couple with bored faces. There were many women, both convict and free, and they kept turning around impatiently to look at the door. Suddenly a person stationed at the door waved and whispered excitedly, "They're coming!" The singers began to clear their throats. A wave of people surged from the door, someone shouted sternly, and finally, the young couple stepped inside. He was a convict typesetter, about twenty-five years old, dressed in a jacket with a stiffly starched wing collar and a white cravat. She was a convict, about three or four years his senior, in a blue dress with white lace and flowers in her hair. A shawl was spread out on the rug. The bridegroom stepped on it first. The best men, typesetters, were also wearing white ties. Father Yegor emerged from behind the altar and spent a long time leafing through the prayer book propped up on the lectern. "Blessed be our God,..." he intoned, and the wedding ceremony began. While the priest was placing wreaths on the bride's and groom's heads and praying to God to crown them with honor and glory, the faces of the women in the congregations expressed deep emotion and joy, and it seemed as if everyone had forgotten that the ceremony was taking place in a prison church, in penal servitude, far, very far from their native land. The priest spoke to the groom, "Exalt yourself, oh bridegroom, as did Abraham...." As soon as the ceremony was finished, the church emptied and the smell of melting wax spread from the burning candles which the guard was rushing to put out, and all at once it became very depressing. We stepped out on the portico. Rain. Close to the church, a crowd had gathered in the darkness and two tarantasses[15] stood by. In one sat the newlyweds; the other was empty.

"Here, Father!" Voices were calling out to Father Yegor and dozens of hands were stretching out of the darkness as if to grab him. "This way, Father! Do us the honor!"

Father Yegor was helped into the tarantass and set off for the home of the newlyweds.

## Visit Cemeteries

*Study the graves and the headstones; notice the inscriptions; take part in a funeral.*

At the Aleksandrovsk cemetery I saw a black cross with an image of the Holy Mother and the following inscription: "Here lie the ashes of the maid Afimya Kurnikovaya, deceased in the year 1888, on the 21st day of May. She was 18 years old. This cross was erected in her memory and to mark the departure of her parents to the mainland in the year 1889, in June."

…The cemetery was situated about a half-mile from the church, behind the settlement, near the sea, on a steep hill. While we were still climbing the hillside, we were overtaken by the funeral procession. Evidently, the service had taken no more than a couple of minutes. From the top of the hill, we could see the coffin lurching on the stretcher and a little boy holding back and pulling away from a woman who was dragging him by the hand.

On one side, we had an extensive view out on the post and the surrounding countryside; on the other, we saw the sea, peaceful and sparkling in the sun. There were a lot of graves and crosses on the hill. Two large crosses standing side by side marked the graves of a certain Mitsul and the guard Selivanov, who was killed by a prisoner. The small crosses that marked the graves of the convicts were all identical and reticent. While Mitsul will be remembered for some time to come, those others lying under all those little crosses—the murderers, fugitives, chain-clanging prisoners—are of use to no one…except, perhaps, to someone out in the Russian steppe, or to some old drayman sitting by a campfire deep in a forest somewhere, trying to relieve his boredom by telling a story about a man from his village who had once gone on a crime spree. His companion stares out into the darkness and shivers; a night bird shrieks—that is the extent to which he will be remembered. A cross marking the grave of an exiled medic is inscribed as follows:

> *Passer-by! May this verse to you recall*
> *That all beneath the skies is finite, etc.*

And closes with:

> *Farewell, my comrade, till that joyful morn!*
> *Ye. Fedorov*

## Keep Moving

*Fight the fatigue that comes with research by moving around.*

On September 10, I was back on the *Baikal*, with which the reader is already acquainted, this time to sail to the south of Sakhalin Island. I was pleased to be going because I had grown quite tired of the north and was anxious for new impressions. The *Baikal* hoisted anchor shortly after nine. It was very dark. I stood alone at the stern, looking back, saying farewell to that gloomy little world guarded from the sea by the Three Brothers now barely visible above the surface of the water and looming in the darkness like three black monks. Even through the din of the ship, I could hear the ominous crash of waves against those reefs. Soon, however, Zhonkier and the Brothers fell far behind and vanished—for me, forever—in the darkness. The tumult of the turbulent waves, filled with an impotent, evil yearning, slowly faded.... [16]

We had sailed about six miles when fires flared up on the shore: this was the frightful Voyevodsk prison; a little farther along, we caught sight of the fires of Dué. Then, a bit later on, everything disappeared, and only the darkness remained and with it, the sort of dread with which one wakes up from a portentous nightmare.

# OBSERVE

## Make Tours of Inspection

*Visit sites at times suitable for seeing how they normally function.*

I arrived at five o'clock in the morning, just as the settlers were getting up. What stench, filth, crowding! Their hair was disheveled as though they had spent the night brawling; their faces, still half-asleep, were sallow and sickly and seemed insane. It was clear that they had slept in their clothes and boots, tightly packed together on the sleeping platform[17] or on the filthy dirt floor beneath it. The physician making the rounds with me that morning told me that there was only seven cubic feet of air for every three or four men. And this, incidentally, at a time when cholera was expected on Sakhalin and all vessels had been placed under quarantine.

That same morning I made a visit to the Voyevodsk prison. It was built in the 1870s on a steep bank of over 3,360 square feet that had to be leveled before the building could be erected. At present, this is the most infamous of all the Sakhalin prisons. It has withstood all attempts at reform and thus serves as a perfect example of the old model of prisons that used to inspire such intense disgust and horror in eyewitnesses. The Voyevodsk prison consists of three large buildings and a smaller one for individual cells. Naturally, there is not much one can say about the cubic volume of air or the ventilation here. When I entered the prison, the floors had just been washed, and the damp, dank air had not yet dissipated since the night and lay heavy. The first thing I heard here were complaints about bedbugs. There is no living for the bedbugs. At one time, they were exterminated with chloride of lime or frozen to death during the severe cold, but nowadays even these measures are useless. The quarters of the prison guards also have the sour stench of the latrine; here too one hears complaints about bedbugs.

## Listen to Rumors

*Listen to gossip and check on sources to verify reliability; try to determine why false rumors receive as much credence as accurate reports.*

The court councilor aside (who is working as a surveyor on Sakhalin)—why is it that the free settlers and the formerly exiled peasants do not return to the mainland when they have a right to do so? One reason appears to be that their agricultural successes keep them on Sakhalin, but this obviously cannot explain all the instances. After all, only some of the settlers use the communal meadows and plow land. Only eight settlers have meadows and cattle; twelve have plow lands, so, no matter how you look at it, the scale of agriculture here is simply not such as to explain its exceptionally fine economic position. There are absolutely no workers for hire, no craftsmen, and only L, a former officer, keeps a shop. There are no official data that might explain why the residents of Sakhalin are wealthy, and so the only way to understand this situation is by considering the one remaining factor: its bad reputation. In the past Slobodka used to have an extremely widespread black market in alcohol. The import and sale of spirits is now strictly forbidden on Sakhalin, and consequently has given rise to a peculiar kind of traffic in contraband. Alcohol was sometimes smuggled onto the island in tin cans shaped like sugar loaves, in samovars, and even in belts, but usually it was simply shipped in barrels and in the usual bottles since the petty officials were on the take, and the higher-ups looked the other way.

One hears that on Sakhalin the climate itself makes women fertile. Old women give birth, and even women who were barren in Russia and had given up all hope of ever bearing children, get pregnant here. The women are said to be in a rush to populate Sakhalin and often produce twins. In Vladimirovka, a middle-aged woman with a grown-up daughter was certain that she was carrying twins because she'd heard so much talk on the subject; she was most disappointed when she was delivered of only one child. "Look some more," she begged the midwife. In fact, however, twin births occur no oftener here than they do in Russia. In the ten-year period ending January 1, 1890, the colony registered 2,275 births of both sexes, as compared to 26 so-called multiple births.[18] All these somewhat hyperbolic rumors about the exceptional fecundity of the women, twins, etc., reveal the degree of interest with which the exiled population regards fertility and its significance for the area.

## Study the Graffiti

*Ask yourself why people write on benches and walls.*

Apparently, there used to be benches on the side of the lighthouse road but they were removed to prevent the convicts and exiles in the area from writing or carving dirty ditties and obscenities on them. To be sure, there are plenty of pornography buffs living in freedom, but when it comes to sheer cynicism, nothing can rival the convicts. Here, not only the messages scrawled on the benches and on backyard fences are vile, but even the love letters are revolting. It strikes me as remarkable that the person who writes obscenities on benches should also at the same time feel lost, rejected, and profoundly unhappy. An old man might say he's sick of life, he might complain that it's time to die, that his rheumatism is killing him and his eyes are failing; but just listen to the gusto with which he lets loose with a string of curses, and hear how he lets fly the choicest obscenities and ornate turns of phrase as he composes intricate incantations against fevers. And if he happens to be literate, he just cannot seem to stifle the urge or resist the temptation to scratch with his fingernails a dirty word into the latrine wall.

## Note the Signs of Social Hierarchy

*Be attentive to formal and informal forms of address, hat doffing, use of space, sartorial details, and bodily marks.*

The guards on duty let the prisoners play cards and themselves take part in the gambling; they drink with the exiles and carry on a trade in liquor.... The exiles have no respect for them and view them with contemptuous indifference. They call them "crackers" to their face and address them with the familiar second-person singular. The administration does not attempt to raise their prestige, probably because it feels this would be useless. The officials address the guards familiarly and speak abusively to them in front of the convicts.... As though ashamed of their duties, the guards from the privileged class look for ways to distinguish themselves from their colleagues: one might wear a slightly wider braid on his shoulders; another might don an officer's cockade; a third, a collegiate registrar,[19] might identify himself in official documents not as "guard" but as "director of works and workers."

While I was in Aleksandrovsk, I saw that the officials and their families occupied the front part of the church during services; next came a colorful row of soldiers' and guards' wives and free women with their children; then came the guards and the soldiers; and at the very back, right up against the rear wall, were the settlers in their city clothes, the convict clerks. May a convict with a shaved head, with one or two stripes down his back, shackled, or with a ball and chain attached to his ankles, go to church if he so desires? A priest to whom I posed this question replied, "I don't know."

In Sakhalin, free citizens do not doff their caps when they enter into the barracks. This courtesy is required only of exiles.

Here corporal punishment is administered more often than in the north and sometimes as many as fifty men are beaten at a time. There is one stupid custom in the south that was introduced by some long-forgotten colonel: when you, a free citizen, happen to run into a group of prisoners on the street or on the shore, from fifty paces away you will hear the guard shouting, "At-ten-tion! Re-move caps!" The bareheaded, gloomy men file past you, cowering, as though fearing that if they had waited to take off their caps at twenty or thirty, rather than fifty, paces, you would have thrashed them with your cane, just like Mr. Z or Mr. N.

## Pay Attention to Place Names

*Consider the significance of place or street names.*

It is the custom on Sakhalin to name streets after living officials.

Beyond Aleksandrovsk, upstream of the Duyka, is the settlement of Korsakovskoye. It was established in 1881 and named in honor of M. S. Korsakov, the former Governor General of eastern Siberia. It is a curious fact that settlements on Sakhalin are named for Siberian generals, jailers, and even medics, while explorers such as Nevelskoy, the navigator Korsakov, Boshniyak, Polyakov, and many others, who, in my opinion, deserve to be commemorated more than someone like that jailer Derbin who was murdered for his cruelty—are forgotten.[20]

The colonists themselves call their settlement "Warsaw" because of its many resident Catholics.

## Note Traces of the Past

*Ask yourself whether the appearance of buildings, house furnishings, and speech patterns might not retain traces of the past, and in what ways they might do so.*

The hut consists of one room with a Russian stove. The floor is made of wood. It contains a table, two or three stools, a bench, and a bed frame with bedding, or the bedding is placed directly on the floor. Sometimes there is no furniture at all except for a featherbed in the middle of the floor, obviously just slept on. A mug of leftovers sits on the windowsill. The furnishings would be more in place in a solitary confinement cell than in a hut or a room. Wherever there are women and children, no matter how poor, it feels homey and somehow reminiscent of peasant life, though, to be sure, one senses the absence of something crucial: there's no grandfather, no grandmother, no old icons, no old furniture. The home has no past, no traditions. There is no icon corner, or, if there is one, it is barren and dim, devoid of votive candle and decorations. There are no customs. The furnishings are haphazard and suggest that the family is transient, that it just moved into the lodgings and has not settled in yet. There is no cat. There is no cricket chirping on a cold winter night.... Worst of all, there is no motherland.

When you ask an old settler whether he remembers any good folk having once lived on the island, he'll stop to reflect, as if trying to recollect something that happened a long, long time ago, and finally say, "There were all kinds." Nowhere is the past forgotten as quickly as it is on Sakhalin, and that is because of the exceeding transience of the convict population, which basically turns over every five years, and because of the lack of accurate record keeping in the local offices. Anything that happened twenty or twenty-five years ago is considered ancient history, forgotten and lost to memory. The only things that survive are a handful of buildings, Mikryukov, a couple of dozen stories, and some statistics from the past, which, however, cannot be trusted because none of the departments had even the faintest idea how many prisoners, fugitives, deceased, etc., might have been on the island.

## Use Your Nose

*Take in smells, identify their source, describe them using plain language, and try to determine their chemical composition.*

After spending the day working, usually in foul weather, the convict returns to the prison for the night. His clothing is sodden, his boots filthy; there is nowhere to dry anything; he hangs some of his clothes on the sleeping platform, the rest he uses for bedding. His sheepskin coat reeks of mutton; his footwear smells of leather and tar. His underwear, permeated with bodily fluids, wet and unwashed, is tossed into a heap along with old sacks and mildewed rags. His footcloths have a suffocating reek of sweat. His body, unwashed, lice-ridden, and flatulent, is addicted to cheap tobacco. Bread, meat, dried fish—which usually he himself salted in prison—crumbs, chunks, bones, and leftover *shchi*[21] all go into his mess tin. He squashes bedbugs with his fingers on the sleeping platform. All this makes for fetid, dank, and sour-smelling prison air. It is so saturated with vapor that during severe frosts, the windows freeze over with a thick layer of ice, making the space dark by day. Hydrogen sulfide, ammonia, and all sorts of other compounds mix with the air and the water vapor, and the result is something that, in the words of one inspector, "sickens the very soul."

## Listen

*Listen to noises, sounds, and background voices.*

It is always quiet in Dué. The ear soon grows used to the measured clang of chains, the roar of the surf, the hum of telegraph wires, and these sounds serve only to reinforce the impression of a dead stillness. The seal of bleakness lies not only on the striped posts. If someone on the street were suddenly to burst out laughing, it would sound harsh and unnatural. From the very beginning of Dué, life here has taken a course that only the most implacably brutal, desperate sounds can convey, and only the savage, bone-rattling blasts that blow in from the sea through the gap on winter nights can sing what must be sung. That is why it is so strange to hear erupting from this silence the singing of Shkandyba, Dué's eccentric. This convict, an old man now, refused to work from the moment he landed on Sakhalin and every conceivable form of coercion failed in the face of his indomitable, downright brutish obstinacy. He was kept in isolation cells, he was flogged, but he stoically endured every form of punishment and after it was over, invariably announced, "I'm not going to work." They took a lot of trouble trying to break him, but finally had to give it up. Now he strolls from one end of Dué to another, singing.

There is a large square in the center of the settlement and on it stands a wooden church and around it there are no shops, as in our villages, but only prison structures, offices, and official lodgings. As you cross the square, you feel like you might be at a noisy fair humming with the voices of Uskovo gypsies trading horses; stinking of tar, manure, and smoked fish; clamorous with the lowing of cows and the screech of accordions and the singing of drunks. But this idyllic fantasy melts into thin air at the first repellent sound of clanging chains and the muffled shuffle of feet as prisoners and guards cross the square on their way back to prison.

## Touch

*Use your sense of touch.*

In fact, the bread was atrocious. When I broke it open, tiny drops of moisture glistened in the sunlight, and it stuck to my fingers and looked like a filthy lump of slime that was repulsive to touch.

## Taste

*Use your sense of taste.*

Tea came with wheat pancakes and sour cream, egg pie, fritters, and sweet buns. The pancakes were thin and greasy; the buns tasted and looked like those yellow, spongy rolls Ukrainians sell in bazaars in Taganrog and in Rostov-on-the-Don…. If you order something warm for lunch, they will always bring "duck soup." This is an unpalatable, murky slop with chunks of wild duck meat and giblets complete with their original contents. It is not just unappetizing: it is downright nauseating.[22]

# COLLECT FACTS

## Consult Written Sources

*Study reports and official decrees, lists, regulations, and private letters; deduce customs from prohibitions that ban them.*

Rumor has it that the people of Sakhalin do well once they move to the mainland. I was able to read their letters, but did not have the opportunity to see how they actually do in their new locations.

Bishops have made frequent visits to Sakhalin, traveling with the same simplicity and putting up with the same discomforts and privations of the road as ordinary priests. During their tours, they organized churches, consecrated various structures, visited prisons, and offered words of consolation and hope to the exiles.[23] The character of their ministry can be appreciated from the following excerpt from a resolution in a letter written by the Most Reverend and preserved in the Korsakov church: "Whereas not all [of the exiles] have faith and repentance, many of them do, as has been ascertained by myself. For nothing save the feeling of repentance and faith had moved them to shed bitter tears when I preached to them in 1887 and 1888. Aside from punishing crime, incarceration has the aim of instilling in prisoners morally sound sentiments, especially to keep them from sinking into despair in their tribulation."

The prisons have many guards, but no order. The guards, as the island commandant has himself recognized, are a constant burden on the administration. Scarcely a day goes by that the daily orders do not levy some penalty or other—a demotion or even discharge: one for unreliability and dereliction of duties; another for immorality, laxness, and stupidity; a third for pilfering government supplies under his care; a fourth for looking the other way; a fifth, not only for failing to maintain order on the barge on which he's been stationed, but even for setting a bad example by stealing walnuts from the same barge; a sixth, for selling government axes and nails; a seventh, for chronic laxness in furnishing feed to government cattle; and eight, for nefarious relations with convicts. From the daily orders, we learn about a senior guard who, while on duty, presumed to break into the women's barracks by climbing in through a window after first having bent back the iron bars, with the intent of pursuing a romantic objective. On another occasion, a guard admitted a colleague, a private in rank, into a cell for the solitary confinement of female prisoners at one o'clock in the morning. The guards do not confine their amorous escapades to the narrow sphere of the women's barracks and individual cells....

In the daily orders we also find mention of violence, insubordination, extreme impertinence toward superiors in the presence of convicts, and, finally, of prisoners' being beaten about the head with batons and sustaining serious injuries.

## Save Receipts, Schedules, and Fliers

*Whenever possible, collect documents, pamphlets, and announcements.*

At noon, I went for a stroll around the village. As I passed into the outskirts, I came across a pretty cottage fronted by a little garden and displaying a small brass plaque above the door. Next to the cottage, sharing the same yard, was a small shop. I went in to buy food. This "Commercial Establishment" and "Commercial Supplies Warehouse"—as the humble enterprise referred to itself in the printed and handwritten pricelists that are still in my possession—belonged to the settler L, a former officer of the Guards whom twelve years earlier the St. Petersburg Regional Court had sentenced to penal servitude for murder. He had completed his sentence and now engaged in trade and in provisioning road construction projects and such. For this he received a senior supervisor's salary. His wife, a free woman and a member of the gentry, worked as a nurse in the prison hospital. The shop sold stars for adorning epaulets, Turkish delight, cross-cut saws, sickles, and "ladies' summer hats in the most fashionable and latest styles from 4 rubles 50 kopecks to 12 rubles each."

One of the convicts gave me a petition entitled: "Confidential. From Our Godforsaken Hole. To the Magnanimous and Gracious Littérateur, Mr. Ch. Whose Visit Gladdened this Unworthy Island of Sakhalin. Post of Korsakov." The following verses, entitled "Wolfbane," were included:

> Most proudly, it grows on the riverbank,
> Surrounded by mud in a hollow:
> A pretty blue leaf midst the reedy rank
> 'Tis medicine's Aconite hallow.
> This wolfbane plant,
> From the Creator's own hand,
> With its fatal appeal
> Many mortals will kill,
> And Abraham's bosom will fill.

## Study the Climate

*Analyze meteorological charts, collect opinions, report your own experiences, make comparisons among different zones; show the impact of weather on the vegetation, harvests, and temperament.*

The mayor of Vladivostok once told me that "there is no such thing as a climate" of Vladivostok or any other area of the eastern seaboard. Sakhalin itself is said to have no climate, only bad weather—the worst in all of Russia—though I personally cannot vouch for the accuracy of this observation. During my sojourn, the summer weather was delightful, contrary to the unusually high precipitation the meteorological charts and various reports had led me to expect.

Winter in the Aleksandrovsk region is more severe than in Archangelsk, spring and summer is like Finland, and autumn is like St. Petersburg. The mean annual temperature is zero degrees, just as on the Solovetsky Islands.[24] There is permafrost in the Duyka valley. Polyakov measured it at 21 inches deep on June 20. On July 14, he reported snow under rubbish heaps and in the hollows near the mountains, and the snow did not melt until the end of the month. On July 24, 1889, snow fell in the mountains, which are low here, and the locals put on their furs and sheepskins. Over a nine-year period, the ice on the Duyka broke on April 23 at the earliest, and on May 6 at the latest. There was not one thaw during the entire nine winters. Temperature fell below freezing 181 days of the year, with cold winds on 151 days. All of this has important practical implications. Gryaznov reports that in the Cherepovetsky district, where summers are warmer and longer, buckwheat, cucumbers, and wheat do not ripen properly, while in the Aleksandrovsk region the local agriculture inspector claims there has never been a year when the number of hot days was sufficient for the oats and wheat to ripen.

The local excessive humidity should be of great interest to agronomists and hygienists. There is precipitation on an average of 189 days per year: snow on 107 days and rain on 82 days. (In the Cherepovetsky district it rains on 81 days and snows on 82 days.) For entire weeks at a time, leaden clouds cover the sky, and the continuously dismal weather seems endless to the natives. This kind of weather leads to oppressive thoughts, despondency, and drinking. Who knows, perhaps its influence has led many cold-blooded people to brutality, and many a good-natured, weak soul has lost all hope of a better life.... Fogs occur frequently, especially on the sea, where they are a curse for sailors; the salty ocean fogs are said to be harmful to vegetation, the trees as well as the grasses, all along the coast.... Once, on a clear day, I saw a white wall of fog moving in from the sea; it was the color of milk, and gave the impression of a white curtain dropping from the sky.

## Take a Census

*When facts are unavailable, it is useful to take a census, not so much to obtain statistics, as to gain access to homes and the chance of meeting people.*

I came up with the only way someone in my position could visit a great many settlements and get to know how people actually live. I undertook a census. In the settlements, I visited all the huts and took down the names of the owners, members of their families, lodgers, and workers. I received a gracious offer of help in the form of assistants who might lighten my load and save time, but since my main objective in taking the census was not the final figures but the impressions produced by the very process, I very rarely accepted help. Consequently, this work that was conducted by a single man over a period of three months can scarcely be called a census; the findings are neither precise nor comprehensive, but even so, given the paucity of substantive data in literature and in the records of the Sakhalin administrative offices, my figures may end up being useful.

## Frame Questions

*Do not solicit answers that already exist in written sources; formulate questions that produce clear responses; separate the answers by gender.*

For the purpose of the census, I ordered index cards at the police department printing shop. The questioning followed a specific sequence. On the first line of each card, I noted the name of the post or settlement. On the second line: the house number as recorded on the prison list of households. Then, on the third line, the status of the interview subject: convict, settler, peasant formerly exiled, free person. I recorded only free persons who were either members of the exile's household through, for example, legal or common-law marriage, or were part of the family, or those who resided with the household as, for instance, laborers or lodgers. Fourth line: given name, patronymic, and surname.[25]... On the same line I noted the relationship of the interview subject to the master of the house: wife, son, female cohabitant, worker, lodger, son of lodger, etc.... Fifth line: age.... The sixth line asked about religion. The seventh: place of birth.... The eighth line: year of arrival in Sakhalin.... On the ninth line, I recorded the main occupation and trade. On the tenth: literacy. This question usually takes the form of: "Are you literate?" Mine, however, asked, "Can you read?" and thus spared me many incorrect answers since peasants who cannot write but can read printed letters usually consider themselves illiterate.... [The eleventh line identified family status: married, widowed, single]... Finally, the twelfth line: "Do you receive public assistance from the state?"... I used a red pencil to draw a line across the cards of female subjects as a simple way of indicating gender.

## Conversation, Not Interrogation

*Have conversations with people you meet on the street, or at work, or visiting over tea.*

While strolling one day along the pier in Aleksandrovsk, I stepped into a boathouse where I found an old man of sixty or seventy and an old woman. They were loaded down with bags and bundles, as if setting off on a journey. We struck up a conversation. The old man had just recently received his peasant rights and was now leaving for the mainland with his wife, first to Vladivostok, and from there, "God knows where." From what they said, I gathered that they had no money. The steamer was scheduled to leave in a day or two, and they had come to the harbor to wait, hiding in the boathouse with all their possessions, and worrying that they might be turned back. They spoke of the mainland with love and reverence, confident that they would find happiness there.

In addition to the railroad and the Slobodka I have just described, the area between the seashore and the post featured an additional curiosity: the ferry across the Duyka. The object floating in the water was neither rowboat nor barge, but a large, perfectly square box. The captain of this unique vessel was a convict by the name of Krasivyj, or "Handsome," "Surname Forgotten." At the age of seventy-one, he was stooped, with jutting shoulder blades, a broken rib, a missing thumb; his body was scarred from years of lashings and beatings. His hair looked faded rather than gray. His clear, blue eyes expressed good-natured merriment. Ragged and barefooted, he was agile, chatty, and laughed with ease. In 1855, after he had deserted from the army "out of stupidity," he became a tramp and started calling himself "Surname Forgotten." He was arrested and packed off to the Tran Baikal, or, as he put it, "to Cossack country."

"Back then, " he told me, " I used to think that people in Siberia live underground, and so I up and ran away straight down the road away from Tyumen. I got as far as Kamyshlov, and there they caught up with me and sentenced me, your worship, to twenty years' penal servitude and ninety lashes. They packed me off to Kara, gave me that lashing, and then moved me from one place to another, to Sakhalin, to Korsakov. I took off from Korsakov with a pal, but we only got as far as Dué. I got sick and had to stop. My pal, meanwhile, got as far as Blagoveshchensk. Now I am on my second term, and it is twenty-two years I have been here on Sakhalin. And my one crime was deserting from the army."

"So why do you hide your real name? What's the point?"

"Last summer I did give my real name to an official."

"So what happened?"

"Nothing happened. The official says, 'By the time we make the correction, you'll be dead. Just stay the way you are. What do you need your name for anyway?' He's right, no mistake about it.... I haven't got much longer to live anyway. Still, my good sir, at least my kin would know my whereabouts."

"What is your name?"

"Here I'm called Ignatyev, Vasily, your excellence."

"And your real name?"

"Handsome" stopped to think for a moment. "Nikita Trofimov. I come from Skopinsky district, Ryazan province."

I got into the box to cross the river. "Handsome" leaned into the long pole and pushed against the riverbed, straining his emaciated, bony body. It was hard work.

"It's hard for you, isn't it?"

"It's nothing, your excellence. No one's breathing down my neck. I take it slow."

He told me that in all his twenty-two years on Sakhalin he was never beaten and never jailed.

"That's because when they send me to saw wood, I go. When they put this pole in my hand, I take it. When they tell me to light stoves in the office, I light them. You've got to submit. Life, no use angering God, is good. Praise the Lord."

Travelers passing through Novo-Mikhailovka cannot avoid running into the formerly exiled peasant Potemkin.... He keeps a shop here and another one in Dué, where his son runs the business. He gives the impression of being a hardworking, intelligent, and prosperous Old Believer.[26] His rooms are clean, hung with wallpaper and a print with the inscription: "Marienbad. Sea Bathing near Libava." Both he and his aged wife are sober, thoughtful, and diplomatic in their remarks. Over tea, they told me that it is possible to make a living on Sakhalin and that the soil is fertile, but— and here's the problem—that the people have gotten lazy, spoiled, and passive. I asked whether the rumor was true that he had once served watermelons and melons from his own gardens to an important personage. Without batting an eye, he answered, "That's correct. Melons do ripen here from time to time."[27]

## Make Inquiries

*Ask for information and explanations.*

Card games are very popular in Upper Armudan and the local players are famous throughout Sakhalin. Short on money, the gamblers of Armudan play for very low stakes, but play vigorously, continuously, just as in the play *Thirty Years, or The Life of a Card Player*.[28] I had the following conversation with a settler named Sizov, one of the most passionate and tireless players in the area.

"Why, your excellence, are we not allowed on the mainland?" he asked.

"And what would you do there?" I teased. "There's no one there for you to play cards with."

"Not at all: that's where the real games are."

"You play shtoss?" I asked after a pause.

"Exactly right, your excellence. I play shtoss."

Later, as I was leaving Upper Armudan, I asked my coachman, a convict:

"Do they play for stakes?"

"For sure, for stakes."

"What do they stand to lose?"

"What do you mean, what? Government rations, bread, for instance, or smoked fish. He'll lose his grub and his clothes, but he'll just keep on sitting there, cold and hungry."

"But what will he eat?"

"What? Well, if he wins, he eats, if he doesn't win, he goes to bed all the same, on an empty stomach."

## Study Children

*Talk with children and observe their games to understand, among other things, the adult world.*

The children watch a gang of prisoners in chains with absolute indifference. When they see shackled convicts pushing a wheelbarrow filled with sand, they jump on the back of the barrow and roar with laughter. They play at prisoners and soldiers. A little boy runs out into the street and shouts at his pals: "Attention!" "Fall back!" Or he bundles up his toys and a piece of bread and tells his mom, "I'm going on the road!" "Watch out, a soldier might shoot you," his mother teases. He goes out on the street and wanders up and down while his pals, pretending to be soldiers, give chase. The children of Sakhalin talk about vagrants, birch rods, whips; they know about things like executioners, shackled prisoners, and cohabitants.

The only person I found at home in one of the huts I was visiting in Upper Armudan was a towheaded boy of about ten with stooped shoulders and bare feet. His pale face was covered with large freckles and seemed to be made of marble.

"What's your father's patronymic?" I asked.

"Dunno," he answered.

"What do you mean? You are living with your father and you don't know his name? Shame on you!"

"He's not my real father."

"What do you mean, not 'real'?"

"He's mom's cohabitant."

"Is your mother married or widowed?"

"Widow. She came here on account of her husband."

"What do you mean, 'on account of her husband'?"

"She killed him."

"You remember your father?"

"No. I'm illegitimate. My mom had me in Kara."[29]

Sakhalin children are pale, skinny, and listless; they wear rags and are always hungry…and generally die of intestinal ailments.

## Quantify

*Count, measure, weigh.*

*Mgachi.* Population: 38, 20 males and 18 females. Homesteaders: 14. Families: 13, of which only 2 are legitimate. Arable land: approximately 32.4 acres, which for the past three years has not been sown with grain, but planted with potatoes. Eleven homesteaders are original settlers, with five of these having gained peasant status. Profits are good, which explains why the peasants are not in a hurry to move to the mainland. Seven keep dog teams, which they use in the winter to move the mail and passengers. One is a professional hunter. As for the fishing mentioned in the records of the central prison administration for 1890, there is none worth noting.

*Tangi.* Population: 19, 11 males and 8 females. Homesteaders: 6. Arable land: approximately 8.1 acres, which, as in Mgachi, where the cultivation of grain is hampered by frequent sea fogs, are planted under potatoes. Two homesteaders own boats and engage in fishing.

*Khoe.* Situated on the eponymous cape that juts prominently into the sea and is visible from Aleksandrovsk. Population: 34, 19 males and 15 females. Homesteaders: 13. Disenchantment has not set in here yet and wheat and barley are still planted. Three are hunters.

*Trambaus.* Population: 8, 3 males and 5 females. It is a happy settlement that has more women than men. Homesteaders: 3.

*Viakhty.* On the Viakhty River, which links the lake with the sea and in this respect recalls the Neva. The lake is said to contain whitefish and sturgeon. Population: 17, 9 males and 8 females. Homesteaders: 7.

*Vangi.* The northernmost settlement. Population: 13, 9 males and 4 females. Homesteaders: 8.

In another ward I found: a convict, his free wife, and son; a convict Tatar woman and her daughter; a convict Tatar, his free wife, and two little Tatar children in skullcaps; a convict, his free wife, and son; a settler—a thirty-five-year veteran of penal servitude, still youthful, with pitch-black whiskers, lacking boots and hence barefoot, a passionate card player[30]—and next to him on the sleeping platform his convict mistress, a shrunken, sleepy, and pitiful-looking creature; next to them, a convict, his free wife, and three children; a bachelor convict; a convict, his free wife, and two children; a settler; a well-groomed, cleanly shaved old convict. A piglet roots around the ward noisily; the floor lies under a slimy filth; the air stinks of bedbugs and something sour; it is said that one cannot live for the bedbugs.

Just how easy it is for the cooks to miscalculate the number of portions is clear from the amounts of each ingredient that go into the pot. On May 3, 1890, 1,279 persons in Aleksandrovsk prison were fed from a single pot into which went: 540 lbs of meat; 200 lbs rice, 50 lbs of flour for thickening, 40 lbs salt, 960 lbs potatoes, 1/3 lb bay leaf, and 2/3 lb pepper. In the same prison on September 29, 675 inmates were fed: 680 lbs fish, 120 lbs groats, 40 lbs flour, 20 lbs salt, 500 lbs potatoes, 1/6 lb bay leaf and 1/3 lb pepper.

In a ten-year period, 170 incidents of death from unnatural causes were recorded for the Orthodox population. Of these, 20 were executed by hanging, 2 were hanged by unknown persons; 27 committed suicide—in northern Sakhalin by gunshot (one while on sentry duty), and in southern Sakhalin, by wolfbane poisoning. Many died of drowning, freezing, of being crushed by trees; one was mauled by a bear. In addition to such causes of death as stroke, heart attack, apoplexy, general paralysis, etc., the church records also show 17 "sudden" deaths, of which more than half were of persons between the ages of 22 and 44, and only one over 50.

I took several loaves of bread—at random—from the many prepared for daily distribution to the prisoners and weighed them and found that each weighed a little over three pounds.

## Make Inventories

*Draw up lists of objects and instruments.*

From this same report, I transcribe excerpts dealing with the hospital inventory. All three infirmaries had the following: gynecological set: 1; laryngoscopes set: 1; maximal thermometers: 2, both broken; "body temperature" thermometers: 9, of which 2 are broken; "high fever" thermometers: 1; trocar: 1; Pravaz syringes: 3, of which 1 needle is broken; pewter syringes: 29; scissors: 9, of which 2 are broken; enema tubes: 34; drainage tubes: 1; large mortar and pestle: 1, cracked; razor strop: 1; cupping jars: 14.

# 5

# THE ACTUAL WRITING

❧

## OVERCOMING INITIAL DIFFICULTIES

### Do Not Put Off Writing

*Write while your impressions are still fresh.*

*Letter to Alexei Suvorin, March 5, 1891*

My work is nowhere near to being finished. If I put it off until May, I will not get to the Sakhalin project until July at the very earliest, which would be dangerous because my impressions of Sakhalin are already evaporating, and I risk forgetting a lot.

### Understand Your Reasons for Not Writing

*Do not preach and do not hide the truth.*

*Letter to Alexei Suvorin, July 28, 1893*

I have been suspecting for a long time that I have been off course, but I have now finally figured out where I have gone wrong. The falseness is in my apparent desire to teach my reader something with my "Sakhalin" and, at the same time, in my hiding something and holding myself back. But as soon as I let myself describe how much of an eccentric I felt myself to be in Sakhalin and what swine those people are, then, at that point, I felt better and my work took off, even though it did turn out a touch humorous.

# GIVE THE BOOK A SHAPE

## The Beginning

*Begin at the point when you arrive at the project site and relate your first impressions.*

On July 5, 1890, I arrived by steamboat at the city of Niko-layevsk, one of the easternmost outposts of our country. Here, about eighteen miles from the sea, the Amur River is extremely wide. It is a majestic and beautiful spot, but the stories about its past, travelers' tales about its savage winters and equally savage traditions, the nearness of the prison camps, and the filthy, dying town itself—all of this instantly kills any inclination to take pleasure in the landscape.

## Tell the Story of the Journey

*Relate the story of the journey from start to finish, describing the places and the events you experienced—even if these have nothing to do with your main argument—because these will help put your recollections in context.*

On the shore, there were several small houses and a church. This was the Aleksandrovsk command post. The commandant, his administrative assistant, and the telegraph operators all lived here. One of the local officials, a boring and bored gentleman who dined with us on the steamship, talked nonstop during dinner, drank up a storm, and regaled us with that stale anecdote about the geese that gorged on brandied cherries, collapsed in an alcoholic daze, were taken for dead, plucked, dumped outside the house, and, when they revived in the morning, found their way home buck naked. The official swore up and down that the incident with the geese took place in De Castries, in his own house.

There is no resident priest at the local church. When needed, he comes from Marinsky. Good weather is as rare here as it is in Nikolayevsk. I have been told that this spring, while a surveying expedition was working in the area, there were only three days of sun in all of May. Just try to work without sunlight!

Two naval ships, the *Bobr* and the *Tungus*, and two torpedo boats were at anchor. I remember another detail: we had just dropped anchor, when the sky turned black, storm clouds piled up, and the sea turned a strange bright-green.

The days were beautiful, with clear skies and a transparency reminiscent of fall weather in Russia. Evenings were spectacular: I remember the horizon in the west flaming up, the dark-blue sea, and a stark, white moon rising from behind the mountains. On evenings such as these, I used to love driving through the valley between the post and the village of Novo Mikhaylovsk; the road ran smooth and even along the tracks of the tiny rail cars and the telegraph lines. Beyond Aleksandrovsk, the valley narrowed, the shadows grew thick, and the gigantic burdocks looked like exotic tropical plants. Dark mountains pressed in from all sides. Flames from burning coal rose into the sky, and beyond them, one could see the glow of distant forest fires. The moon was rising. Suddenly a fantastic apparition caught my eye: along the rails a small platform came gliding toward me, and on it, leaning on a pole, stood the figure of a convict dressed in white. I was gripped by anxiety.

## Structure the Chapters

*After telling the story of the journey itself, treat each topic separately, relegating each to its own chapter.*

In the following chapters I will describe the posts and settlements and the various types of convict labor and the prisons as best I can, given the limitations of my short visit. Convict labor on Sakhalin takes the most varied of forms: it is not specialized within a single area such as gold or coal extraction, but covers all elements of life and encompasses all the settled areas of the island. Forest clearing, construction, marshland draining, fishing, mowing, loading and unloading of cargo—all these varieties of convict labor have merged so seamlessly with the life of the colony that they can be treated as something independent of the island only if viewed from a very rigid perspective, such as penal mining and factory operations.

I will begin with the Aleksandrovsk valley, with the settlements situated along the Duyka River. This valley was chosen for the first settlement on northern Sakhalin not because it had been most thoroughly explored or was thought to best meet the goals of colonization, but at random because it happened to be closest to Dué, where the penal colony was first situated.

Having completed my survey of the settled areas of Sakhalin, I will now turn to the details of life—some important and others less so—that characterize the colony.

## BEING OBJECTIVE

### Identify Your Sources

*Indicate information that comes from secondary sources or from firsthand experience. Footnote sources; give references to further readings in specialized areas; provide biographical data for individuals mentioned in the text; include anecdotes or details that enhance your credibility; give your critical evaluation of secondary sources.*

There are six tiny settlements on the western shore, right above the mouth of the Arkay River. I did not visit any of them, so my information comes from an inventory of homesteads and the baptismal registry.

Until 1875, the Korsakov Post sentry and the military guardhouse occupied the prison compound, which was located in a dark hovel. "Perhaps this sort of crowding is permissible as a punitive measure for convicts," writes Dr. Sintsovsky, "but a military guard is another matter altogether and there is no known reason why he should be obliged to undergo the same punishment."[1]

From a purely hunting point of view, vertebrates are abundant on Sakhalin. From a commercial point of view, sable, fox, and bear are the most valuable among the fur-bearing animals that are found here in the greatest numbers.[2]

The second village is Mitsul'ka, named in honor of M. S. Mitsul'.[3]

In addition, here I made the acquaintance of Major Sh., the Korsakov prison warden, who had formerly served in the St. Petersburg police force under General Gresser. Sh. was a tall, fleshy man with the solid, imposing carriage that I have observed to be characteristic of local and regional police officers. When he was telling me about all the famous writers of St. Petersburg with whom he was on friendly terms, the major referred to them simply as Misha, Vanya, etc. And when he invited me to lunch and dinner, he twice—entirely without leave—addressed me with the familiar "you" form.[4]

## Ascertain Reliability

*Understand the premises and biases of the source material.*

The statistics on non-Russian, indigenous peoples are compiled by bureaucrats who not only lack the necessary educational or professional credentials, but also are not given any instructions or guidelines on how to carry on their work. When they set about collecting data locally—in the Ghiliak settlements, for instance—they are heavy-handed and rude and impatient in their dealings with the gracious Ghiliaks, whose notion of courtesy does not include arrogance and force, and whose abhorrence of surveys and registrations of any kind calls for exceptional skill and tact and tact on the part of the interviewer.

Before entering the service, the overwhelming majority of bureaucrats who were put in charge of the agricultural colony were neither landowners nor peasants, and were utterly ignorant in matters pertaining to agriculture. In compiling their reports, they invariably fell back on data collected by their inspectors. For their part, local agronomists either lacked training and did nothing; or produced outrageously biased reports; or, straight from the classroom, limited their research to purely theoretical and formal aspects of the problem; or, finally, used the data that was compiled by junior clerks for the use of other offices. One would think it would be possible to obtain solid information from the very people who did the plowing and sowing, but even this source turned out to be unreliable. Afraid of losing their subsidies or of jeopardizing their ability to buy seed grain on credit or of being sentenced to spending the rest of their lives on Sakhalin, the exiles usually underreported their harvests and the amount of land under cultivation.

## Make Comparisons

*Juxtapose material from the most diverse sources, including your own experiences.*

The agricultural inspector's report includes a table on harvest yields for the past five years that is based on data the island commandant considers "sheer fabrication." The figures suggest that the median grain yield is three to one per unit of tilled land. This may be corroborated by another figure: in 1889, the grain yield averaged some 440 pounds per adult, which would represent a threefold yield on planted grain.

When our conversation touched on this subject, Mr. Kamorsky, the Prison Inspector of the Amur region, confirmed that the administration has no right to keep an exile in settler status for any longer than ten years, or to make the granting of peasant status contingent upon any conditions whatsoever. Nevertheless, on Sakhalin I had occasion to meet old men who had spent considerably more than ten years living in the settlements and had not yet received peasant standing. However, I was not able to verify their claims against the official records and so cannot vouch for their accuracy.

In 1872, Sinel'nikov, the Governor-General of eastern Siberia, banned the use of criminals as servants. Nevertheless, even though it still has the force of law, this ban is circumvented in the most flagrant manner. The Collegiate Registrar assigns half a dozen convicts to work as his personal servants, and when he organizes a picnic, he sends an advance party of ten convicts with all the provisions. General Gintse and General Kononovich, island commandants, did fight against these kinds of abuses, but not energetically enough. I found only three orders—at the very most— bearing on the question of servants, and even these were written in such a way that anyone especially keen on it could easily interpret them in his favor.... At any rate, when I was on Sakhalin in 1890, all officials—even those with no connection with the prison administration (for instance, the director of the post and telegraph office)—flagrantly exploited convict labor for their private use. Furthermore, the salaries and the cost of feeding these convict servants were paid out of the government treasury.

If one were to go by the settlement supervisor's figures for the list of homesteads, one might be tempted to conclude that all three Arkovo [settlements] have made tremendous strides in agriculture in the brief period of their existence.... In point of fact, however, this is not the case. All three Arkovos are among the poorest settlements in northern Sakhalin. They might have arable land; they might have cattle; but they have yet to produce a harvest.

## Explain Discrepancies Between Questions and Answers

*Sometimes the most interesting answers can be those that are incorrect or approximate, or even not answers at all.*

To the question "What are you?" the settler usually answers, "A free man." After a decade or, given the right circumstances—as defined by legislation pertaining to exile—after six years, the settler's status changes to "peasant, former exile." To the same question, the peasant answers with dignity—as if he should not be lumped together with any others but is distinctive in some way—"I am a peasant." However, he does not add the qualification "former exile."... Except for soldiers, none [of the former exiles]—be they petty bourgeois, shopkeepers, or clergy—volunteer their most recent status, as if this were already forgotten; instead, they identify their former status in a single word: "free." Asked about their past, they usually preface their answer with the phrase "When I was free."…Occasionally, when asked his name, a 100 percent Russian Orthodox peasant will answer, in all seriousness, "Karl." He might turn out to be a vagrant who had traded names with a German he might have met on the road. I jotted down two such cases: Karl Langer and Karl Karlov.… Women over forty have a hard time giving their age and have to think hard before answering. Armenians from Yerevan province never know their age. One said to me, "Thirty, maybe, or maybe even fifty by now." In cases like these, I had to estimate the age by appearance and then verify it against the record. Youngsters fifteen or older usually say they are younger. A young woman who's already engaged or who has been working as a prostitute for quite some time, will nevertheless give her age as thirteen or fourteen. The reason for this is that poor families receive government rations for children and adolescents below the age of fifteen, and so self-interest prompts them to lie.… Line eight: "In what year did you arrive on Sakhalin?" The answer rarely came without much deliberation. The year of one's arrival on Sakhalin was always a year of terrible misfortune; and there is always the possibility that they may not know the year or may have forgotten it. Ask an old convict woman when she came to Sakhalin and she will answer apathetically, without even thinking, "Who knows? Must have been in '83." Her husband or lover interrupts. "What are you blathering? You came in '85." "So, all right, maybe it was '85," she sighs. We start to calculate, and it turns out the man was right. The men are not as apathetic as the women, but they take a long time in coming up with an answer. They ponder and consult with each other.

"What year were you brought to Sakhalin?" I ask a settler.

"I was in the same convoy as Gladky," he answers, unsure of himself and looking over at his pals.

Gladky came with the first convoy, and the first convoy, that is, the first *Dobrovolets*,[5] came to Sakhalin in 1879. I write down that date. Alternatively, the answer will go as follows: "I spent six years in forced labor, now I'm in my third year as settler... so, you figure it out."

"In other words, you've been on Sakhalin for nine years?"

"No way. I spent two years in the central prison before I came to Sakhalin."

And so it goes. Or here's another answer: "I came the same year Derbin was killed." Or, "That was when Mitsul' died."... "How are we supposed to know? What do you take us for, scholars?" And only after being pressed will they finally admit, "Well, I used to be able to make out print, but now, you know, I forgot how to do it. We're a bunch of ignoramuses, peasants." The blind or nearly blind also call themselves illiterate.

## Cite Documents

*By way of example, transcribe or reproduce written documents.*

A guard, usually an illiterate, low-ranking member of the local command, is posted in each settlement. He reports to visiting officials that everything is in order, keeps an eye on the settlers, and makes sure that they do not leave without permission or fall behind in their agricultural work. He is the settlement's nearest thing to an official, often the only judge, and his reports to the administration provide crucial documentation that is used in evaluating the settler's conduct as homesteader and settler. Here is an example of a guard's report:

List of Inhabitants of the Village of Upper Armudan Reported for Misconduct:

| Surnames and given names | Note why in particular |
| --- | --- |
| 1. Izdugin, Anany | Thief |
| 2. Kiselev, Pyotr Vasil'ev | Ditto |
| 3. Glybin, Ivan | Ditto |
| 4. Galynsky, Semyon | Negligent of home and obstinate |
| 5. Kazankin, Ivan | Ditto |

## Do Not Preach

*Tell things as they are; report the facts so readers may form their own opinions and reach their own conclusions.*

According to the island commandant, "…investigations are undertaken on insufficient grounds, conducted in a desultory and incompetent manner, and the suspects in question are detained without cause." The suspect or the accused is taken under guard and jailed. When a settler was murdered in Goly Mys, four men were arrested and detained in dark, cold cells.[6] Several days later three of them were released, and one was retained in custody. He was put in shackles and was given a hot meal only once every three days. Then, in response to a guard's complaint, he was given one hundred strokes of the lash, and was kept in the dark, intimidated, and deprived of food until he confessed. During this time a free woman, Garanina by name, was also in prison under suspicion of having murdered her husband. She too was locked up in a dark cell and a hot meal every third day. When one of the officials was interrogating her in my presence, she complained that she had been sick for a long time but that for some reason she had not been permitted to see a physician. When the official asked the guard in charge of the cells why he had not bothered to call in a doctor, this was his reply, verbatim, "I did report this to the honorable warden, but he said, 'Just let her croak.'"

This inability to differentiate between preliminary detention (in the dungeon of the penal prison, no less) and incarceration, or to distinguish between free citizens and convicts astonished me all the more since the local district commander was a law school graduate, while the prison warden was a former member of the St. Petersburg police force.

Another time, early in the morning, the district commander and I were visiting the prison cells when the four exiles who had been suspected of murder were released from their cells. They were shaking from cold. Garanina was in her stocking feet, without shoes, and was shivering and squinting in the light. The district commander had ordered that she be moved to a cell with light. Quite by chance, I then happened to notice a man, a Georgian, hovering outside the cell doors like a shadow. He had been sitting there, in the dark passageway, for the past five months, detained on suspicion of having poisoned someone and waiting for the completion of an investigation that had not even been undertaken yet.

In order to meet its obligations and safeguard the interests of the company, the treasury maintains two prisons not far from its mines, one at Dué and another at Voyevodsk, and supports a military presence of 340 men, at an annual cost of about 150,000 rubles.... For its part, the company has to meet three serious obligations: it must develop the Dué mines and support a mining engineer to oversee their proper exploitation; it must make semiannual payments for the coal and the lease of convict labor; it must make exclusive use of convict labor in all aspects of mining operations. These three obligations exist only on paper and have apparently been long since forgotten.

## Voice Your Opinion

*If you do not like something, say so.*

It is just about impossible to say anything in favor of communal jail cells. The inmates of a communal jail cell do not make up a commune or a cooperative of members with individual obligations, but a mob in which no one person bears any responsibility for the space, its occupants, or their belongings. It is utterly impossible to forbid inmates from tracking in mud and filth on their boots, from spitting on the floor, from spreading lice. If there is a stench in the cell, or rampant thieving, or lewd singing, everyone is at fault, which is to say: no one is at fault. I asked a convict who had once been a respectable citizen, "Why are you so slovenly?" "Because," he replied, "here my being neat would be pointless." And indeed, what would be the point of his being clean if on the morrow a new group of convicts is moved into the cell and his new bunkmate is crawling with bugs and stinks to high heaven?

The communal cell deprives inmates of the privacy to pray, think, or be introspective that, according to advocates of the penal system, is essential to meeting the goal of reforming criminals. Instead, the exhausted worker is kept awake all night long by violent games of cards which are tolerated by corrupt guards; his nerves are frayed by the constant cursing, the coarse laughter, the gossiping, the din of slamming doors and the clanging of chains that go on through the night so that his digestion and his psyche cannot but suffer. It is a well-established fact that this brutish, herdlike existence—with its crude diversions and the inevitably pernicious effect of the depraved on the good—has the most debilitating impact on the morale of the inmate. Bit by bit it erodes his capacity for domestic life, that single most important trait he must preserve if, after his release, the inmate is to become a self-sufficient member of the colony in which he is required, by law and under threat of punishment, to take his place as a good householder and a kind family man from the very first day of his residence.

From these barbaric premises and practical arrangements, where fifteen-and sixteen-year-old girls are forced to sleep next to convicts, the reader can draw his own conclusions about the disrespect and contempt that are heaped upon the women and children who voluntarily follow their husbands and fathers into penal servitude, about the low value placed on them, and the negligible amount of thought given to the welfare of the agricultural colony!

## BEING TRUTHFUL

### Portraits

*Describe what people look like.*

Of the women kept in solitary confinement, one in particular draws attention to herself. This is the notorious Sophia Bluvshtein, the "Little Gold Hand" who was sentenced to three years of penal servitude for attempting to escape from Siberia. Small, slim, and graying, she has the creased face of an old woman. Her hands are chained together. On her plank bed, a meager, gray sheepskin serves her as coat and bedding in one. She paces her cell from end to end and seems to be constantly sniffing the air, like a mouse in a trap. Even her expression has something of the mouse about it. Looking at her one finds it hard to believe that until just recently she was such a beauty that she could charm her jailers, as happened in Smolensk, for example, where her guard not only helped her escape but even ran off with her.

In Mitsul'ka lives the sixteen-year-old Tanya, the Gretchen[7] of Sakhalin, daughter of the settler Nikolayev from Pskov province. She is blond and trim, with refined, soft, and gentle features. She is already engaged to marry one of the guards. Whenever I happened to pass through Mitsul'ka, I would always see her sitting at her window, thinking. What could this young, lovely girl who ended up in Sakhalin possibly be thinking, what could she possibly be dreaming—that is something only God can tell.

The son of the Archpriest K. was sentenced for murder, escaped to Russia, committed another murder, and was sent back to Sakhalin. One morning I happened to catch a glimpse of him in the crowd of convicts that was milling around the mine entrance. Dreadfully emaciated, stooped, with dull eyes, in an old summer jacket and ragged trousers worn inside out, shivering in the morning frost, he walked up to the guard who was standing next to me, took off his cap from his balding head, and began to ask for something or other.

## Settings

*Evoke the situation, complete with characters, ambience, and background.*

When I was in Debrinskoye, the convicts were out catching fish for the prison. General Kononovich, the commandant of the island, ordered the settlers to assemble and berated them for selling the prison fish that was not fit to eat. "The convict is your brother and my son," he said to them. "When you cheat the treasury, you cheat your own brother and my own son." The settlers made a semblance of agreeing with him, but their faces suggested that next year both brother and son would be back to eating rotten fish.

In another hut, I witnessed the following scene. A young, dark-haired convict in an elegant shirt and with an unusually sad expression on his face was sitting at the table holding his head in his hands. Meanwhile, the housekeeper, a convict, was picking up the samovar and cups. To my question about his marital status, the young man replied that his wife and daughter had voluntarily come after him to Sakhalin, but that two months ago both had left for Nikolayevsk and were refusing to come back, even though he had written them several telegrams. To this the housekeeper added, "She won't ever come back. She is young. She is free. What is there for her here? She took off, like a bird, and she is gone, lock, stock, and barrel: not like you or me. If I had not killed my husband and if you had not set fires, we would also be free, you and me. But instead, here we are; and you can just go on sitting here and waiting for the wind to bring your little wife back, and you can drown your heart in sorrow...." The young man is suffering. There seems to be a big weight on his soul, but the housekeeper just keeps at him, needling and nagging. I leave the hut, but I can still hear her needling him.

I took part in a prison fishing expedition in Debrinskoye on August 25. The relentless rain cast a melancholy spell on nature; it was difficult to walk along the slippery bank. First, we stopped at a shed where sixteen convicts were salting fish under the supervision of Vasilenko, who had been a fisherman in Taganrog. They had already put up 150 barrels, or about 40 tons. One had the impression that if Vasilenko had not happened to end up in jail, they would not have known what to do with the fish. On the slope between the shed and the bank, six convicts were using very sharp knives to gut the fish and were throwing the entrails into the river; the water was red and murky. The air was heavy with the stench of fish, mud, and blood. Off to the side, a group of convicts, drenched, barefoot or in clogs, was casting a small net.

How do the prisoners eat? There are no mess halls. At noon, the inmates queue up by the barracks or the cooking shed just as if they were buying train tickets. Each one is carrying some kind of container. By now, the soup is thoroughly overcooked and is kept at a simmer in large covered pots. The cook wields a long pole with a scoop bound to its end and uses this as a ladle to dole out portions: two servings of meat at one go or none at all, just as he pleases. By the time the last person in line reaches him, the soup is no longer recognizable as such. All that is left is a kind of gluey, lukewarm glop on the bottom of the pot that has to be thinned with water. After receiving their portions, the inmates scatter. Some eat standing up; others sit on the ground or on their sleeping platforms.

## INSERT YOURSELF INTO THE SCENE

### Reflect on What Is Happening

*Keep in mind that the investigator is also the object of observation.*

"Attention! On your feet!" the guard shouts.

We step into the cell. It appears to be spacious, about 1,400 cubic feet in volume, and it is filled with light. The windows are open. The walls are dark, unpainted, riddled with splinters, with oakum stuffed into the cracks between the logs; only the tile stoves are white. The flooring is unpainted, dried-out wood. Down the length of the cell runs a sleeping platform whose two sides slope up toward the middle to accommodate the sleepers in two rows, head to head. The convicts' spaces are not numbered or marked off in any way, which makes it possible to accommodate anywhere between 70 and 170 inmates. There is no bedding. The men sleep on the bare wood or on old, torn sacks, clothing, or all sorts of disgusting, rotting rags. The sleeping platform is littered with caps, footwear, chunks of bread, empty milk bottles stopped up with bits of paper or rag, boot trees; the space under the platform is packed with small trunks, filthy sacks, bundles, tools, and old rags. A fat cat promenades around the platform. Clothing, pots, and tools hang from the walls and the shelves are full of teapots, bread, and some sort of storage boxes....

Keeping our caps on our heads, we walk the length of the platform bed while the inmates stand at attention and silently study us. We are silent as well and study them, and it almost seems as if we might have come here to buy them.

A shop here is run by a retired sergeant major who used to be a district inspector in the Tymovsk district. He sells groceries and carries copper bracelets and canned sardines as well. He must have taken me for some very important official because the moment I walked into the shop he instantly and without any provocation on my part confided that he had once been mixed up in some shady business but had come out of it clean, and quickly produced testimonials to the effect, among them a letter from a certain General Schneider that concluded, as I recall, with the following sentence, "And when it gets warmer, heat up the melted snow." Then, to prove that he owed nothing to anyone, the sergeant major started rummaging among his documents for some receipts, which he did not end up finding, and I left the shop thoroughly convinced of his innocence and in possession of a pound of plain caramels, for which he had charged me the outrageous price of fifty kopecks.

## Share Your Emotions

*When describing an episode in which you were a participant, describe the emotions you experienced.*

I witnessed a flogging in Dué. The vagrant Prokhorov, originally Myl'nikov, a man of about thirty-five or forty, had broken out of Voyevodsk prison, made himself a small raft, and set off for the mainland. He was spotted from the beach, and a cutter was promptly dispatched to pick him up. The investigation into his escape got under way; official records were consulted and it suddenly emerged that this Prokhorov, originally Myl'nikov, had been convicted for the murder of a Cossack and his two nieces a year ago, and had been sentenced by the Khabarovsk District Court to ninety lashes and the wheelbarrow shackle.[8] Due to an oversight, this sentence had not been carried out. Had Prokhorov not taken it into his head to escape, the oversight might not have become known and he would have been spared the flogging and the shackles, but now the punishment was inescapable. On the morning of the appointed day, August 13, the warden, the physician, and I make our way to the office. Prokhorov, whose arrival has been announced the day before, is sitting on the porch under guard, oblivious of what lies in store for him. When he catches sight of us, however, he gets to his feet, and apparently realizes what is about to happen because his face goes white.

"Into the office!" the warden commands.

We go into the office. Prokhorov is brought in. The physician, a young German, orders him to undress, and listens to his heart to determine how many strokes the prisoner can tolerate. He reaches his decision in less than a minute and then in a businesslike manner sits down to write out his report.

"Ach, the poor fellow!" he mutters dolefully in a Russian heavily accented with German, and dips his pen in the inkpot. "The shackles are too heavy for you! Why don't you just ask Mr. Warden, and he'll order them removed?"

Prokhorov says nothing. His lips are white and trembling.

"It's no use punishing you," the physician continues. "You're all of you hopeless. Such unreliable people in Russia! Ach, you poor, poor fellow!"

The report is completed and added to the file of the investigation into the escape. A heavy silence sets in. The clerk is writing, the doctor and the warden are writing.... Prokhorov still has no idea why exactly he was brought here: on account of his attempted escape, or the old business or both the escape and the old business? This uncertainty oppresses him.

"What did you dream last night?" the warden finally asks him.

"I forgot, your worship."

"Now listen up," says the warden glancing at the official documents. "On such-and-such a day of such-and-such a year the Khabarovsk District Court sentenced you to ninety lashes for murdering a Cossack.... And today is the day you must get them."

And, slapping the prisoner on his forehead, the warden lectures him:

"Why is all this necessary? Why? Because you, you numbskull, want to be smarter than you really are. You keep trying to escape, you think it's going to be better, but it turns out even worse."

We all file into the guardhouse, an old, gray, barracks-like structure. The army medic who is stationed by the door speaks up in a pleading voice, as if he were begging for alms:

"Your worship, if you please, may I have permission to see how they punish a prisoner?"

In the middle of the guardroom stands a sloping bench with openings for securing the arms and legs. The executioner, Tolstykh[9]—a tall, fleshy man with the build of a circus weightlifter, wearing a shirt and an unbuttoned waistcoat—nods to Prokhorov, who silently lies down. Taking his time, Tolstykh silently pulls the prisoner's trousers down to his knees and slowly begins to secure his arms and legs to the bench. The warden stares out the window impassively, while the doctor paces back and forth. He is holding a vial of some sort of medicinal drops in his hands.

"Maybe you want a glass of water?" he asks.

"For the love of God, yes sir, your worship."

At last, Prokhorov is secured. The executioner picks up the lash with three leather tails and slowly unfurls it.

"Buckle up!" he says softly, and without even drawing back his arm, as though just taking aim, he brings the lash down on the prisoner's back.

"O...n...e!" says the warden in the voice of a deacon chanting prayers.

For the first instant Prokhorov is silent and the expression on his face does not change. Then a spasm of pain runs across his entire body, and is followed by something that is not a scream, but more like a shriek.

"Two!" shouts the warden.

The executioner stands to the side and strikes in such a way that the lash falls across the body. Every five strokes he slowly moves over to the opposite side and gives the prisoner a break of about half a minute. Prokhorov's hair is glued to his forehead, his neck is swollen; after the first five or ten strokes, his body, already full of scars from previous floggings, turns purple and blue; his skin splits under each stroke.

"Your worship!" The words break through the shrieks and the wails. "Your worship! Have mercy, your worship!"

After twenty or thirty strokes, Prokhorov begins to whine like someone in a drunken stupor or a delirium:

"I am a wretch, I am a broken man...why are you beating me?"

Then comes a strange sort of stretching of the neck, sounds of retching.... Prokhorov says nothing, but only bleats and wheezes; it seems as if an eternity has passed since the flogging has begun, but the warden keeps on shouting, " Forty-two! Forty-three!" Ninety is a long way off. I go outside. The street is silent and it seems to me that the heartrending sounds from within the guardhouse can be heard in every corner of Dué. A convict dressed in the clothes of a freeman walks by me, glances furtively at the guardhouse, and suddenly every feature of his face and even his gait register horror. I go back into the guardhouse, and then I leave again, and still the warden keeps on counting.

At last: ninety. Prokhorov is quickly untied from the bench and is helped up. The area of his body where the lash landed is livid with bruises and is bleeding. His teeth are chattering. His face is yellow and damp. His eyes are rolling in his head. When he is given the medicinal drops to drink, he convulsively bites down on the glass.... His head is wetted down and he is led off to the infirmary.

"That was for the murder. He'll get another one for escaping," I am told on our way home.

"I love to watch floggings!" the army medic exclaims joyfully, very pleased with himself for having gotten his fill of the abominable spectacle. "I love it! They are such scoundrels, such scum....They should be strung up!"

## Present Your Survey Findings

*The significance of a survey consists in the impressions you collect in the process of conducting it. A good way to present your findings is to describe the way the survey evolved.*

I went from hut to hut unaccompanied. On occasion, however, a convict or a settler who, out of sheer boredom, had taken it on himself to act as my guide joined me. Sometimes I was shadowed, quite close or from a distance, by an armed guard. He was assigned to follow me just in case I needed something explained. Whenever I turned to him with a question, his forehead would instantly break out in a sweat and he would answer, "How could I possibly know that, your worship?" Usually my companion, barefoot and bareheaded and carrying my inkpot, would run ahead, noisily throw open the doors, and hurry to whisper something to the master of the house—most likely his suppositions about the objectives of my survey....

The convict population took me for an official and viewed my census as just another one of those formalities that were so common in the area and only rarely amounted to anything. By the way, the fact that I was not a local—not a Sakhalin official—excited a certain degree of curiosity among the convicts. They would ask me,

"What are you taking all this information down for?"

They came up with all sorts of explanations. Some thought the higher-ups were researching ways to distribute aid to the convicts; others speculated that the decision had finally been made to move everyone to the mainland (according to a persistent and firm conviction circulating on the island, the authorities were always on the verge of moving the penal colony and the settlers to the mainland); yet another group, the self-styled skeptics, said they no longer expected anything good for themselves because God himself had turned His back on them, but they said this mainly to get me to contradict them. And then, from either the doorway or the top of the stove,[10] as if mocking all these hopes and speculations, a voice would be raised, filled with fatigue, boredom, and irritation at being disturbed:

"They go on writing, and writing, and writing, Holy Mother of God!"

## Report Stories from Life

*Collect autobiographical narratives and select one to reproduce as an example of how such tales are told; give examples of the questions that were posed and describe the context in which the stories were shared and the conversations took place.*

Sometimes, while reading or writing, I would suddenly hear a kind of rustling and wheezing sound, and I would feel something heavy moving under my desk by my feet. I would look up to see Yegor, in his bare feet, picking up scraps of paper under the desk or sweeping the floor. In his late thirties, he was an ungainly and awkward fellow—a clumsy oaf, in short—with a simple and, at first glance, stupid face and a mouth as wide as a burbot's. He had red hair, a wispy beard, and tiny eyes. He never answered questions without first giving you a sidelong glance and asking, "How's that?" or, "Who's that?" He addressed me as "your worship" but used the familiar "you." He was incapable of sitting for longer than a minute and was always working and finding something to do. He would be talking with you, but all the time his eyes would be looking around for something to clean or repair. At night, he never slept more than two or three hours because he had no time for sleeping. On holidays he usually stationed himself on a street corner, dressed in a red shirt and a jacket, and stuck out his belly and planted his feet wide apart. This was his version of "going out on the town."

Here, in penal servitude, he had built himself a hut, made buckets, tables, and crude trunks. He could make all kinds of furniture, but only "for himself," meaning, for his own use. He never got into fights and he was never beaten, except for that one time when he was a kid and his father whipped him for letting the rooster into the pea patch he was supposed to have been watching.

One day we had the following conversation:

"Why were you sent here?" I asked.

"What's that, your worship?"

"Why were you sent to Sakhalin?"

"For murder."

"Tell me the whole story, from the beginning."

Yegor leaned against the door, put his hands behind his back, and began his tale.

# WRITING ADVICE

## Write as if You Were Painting

*Imagine that you are painting a picture with all the details and colors.*

If a landscape painter were to visit Sakhalin, I would recommend he make an excursion to Arkovo valley. In addition to its beautiful location, this spot is so unusually rich in color that it is hard to describe without resorting to that stale simile of the multicolored carpet or kaleidoscope. Consider the lush, verdant growth of giant burdocks glistening from the recent rain; beyond them, in a tiny plot no more than twenty-one feet wide, rye is turning green, and beyond that lies a patch of barley, and then burdocks again, and then another patch filled with oats, and then a row of potatoes and two stunted sunflowers with drooping heads, and then a wedge of rich green hemp, and, here and there, umbrella plants thrust their bracts proudly like the arms of candelabra, and scattered throughout this riot of color are rose, vermillion, and crimson patches of poppies. On the road, you pass peasant women wrapped in big burdock leaves to keep off the rain and looking like huge green beetles. And on either side, there are mountains—not the Caucasus, to be sure, but mountains nonetheless.

He is Ukrainian by birth, and a former law student by training. He is young, under forty, which, by the way, is the average age of Sakhalin officials. Times have changed: nowadays officials in the Russian penal system tend to be young rather than old so that if, let's suppose, an artist were to paint the flogging of a beggar, he would have to replace the traditional figure of the old alcoholic captain with his purple nose and paint instead a young man dressed in a smart new uniform.

## Use Photographs

*When describing a place, a situation, or a person, keep a photograph in front of you.*

I have seen elderly inmates rush to hide their chains under the hems of their coats in the presence of a stranger. I have a photograph of a group of chained convicts in a work gang from Dué and Voyevodsk that shows them trying to stand in such a way that their chains would not be visible in the picture.

## Report Conversations

*Use direct discourse to report a conversation.*

This incident took place at nightfall. Two Ghiliaks, one with a goatee, the other with a pudgy, matronly face, were lying on the grass in front of a settler's hut. I was passing by. They called me over and set about entreating me to go into the hut and retrieve the coats they had left with the settler earlier in the day; they themselves were afraid to go in. I pointed out that I also had no right to enter a stranger's house when the owner was not present. They fell silent.

"You a politico? (meaning, 'political prisoner')?" asked the Ghiliak with the matronly face.

"No."

"Then you're a writy-writy (meaning, 'a clerk')?" he asked, looking at the piece of paper I was holding.

"Yes, I write."

"How much money do you make?"

I was making about three hundred rubles a month. That is the figure I gave them. One had to be there to see the unpleasant, even painful impression my answer produced. Both Ghiliaks instantly clutched their stomachs and, leaping to the ground, began to writhe as if in the throes of a horrendous stomachache. Their faces spoke of a profound despair.

"Oh, why do you talk like that?" I made out. "Why do you say such a terrible thing? Oh, that is so bad! You must not do that!"

"But what did I say that was so bad?" I asked.

"Butakov, the regional superintendent, he's a big shot, he gets two hundred, but you—you're no sort of superintendent, you're an itty-bitty writy-writy—and you get three hundred! You said such a bad thing! You must not do that!"

I started explaining that the regional superintendent may indeed be a big shot, but he makes only two hundred because he spends all his time sitting in one place; while I, though a puny writy-writy, I had come here from far, far away, over seven thousand miles away, and my expenses were much bigger than Butakov's and consequently I had to make a lot more money. This explanation seemed to mollify the

Ghiliaks. They looked at each other, held a brief consultation in their native language, and relaxed. Their faces showed that I had now gained their total trust.

"True enough, true enough," the bearded Ghiliak said briskly. "Good. Move along."

"True enough," nodded the other. "Go on."

## Tell Stories as They Were Told

*Tell the stories that were told to you in the words of the original speakers, or try switching between their voices and yours.*

On the eve of the execution, the priest keeps vigil with the condemned man, preparing him for his final journey throughout the night. The preparation consists of a confession and a conversation. One of the priests told me the following:

"Once, at the beginning of my mission, when I was only twenty-five, I was sent to the Voyevodsk prison to prepare two men sentenced to death by hanging. They had murdered a settler for one ruble and forty-four kopecks. I went into their cell and being new to the situation, lost my nerve. I asked the guard to keep the door open and stand outside. But they said,

"'Don't be afraid, reverend. We won't kill you. Sit down, please.'

"I asked: where should I sit? They pointed to the sleeping platform. I took a seat on the water barrel and then, screwing up my courage, I moved to sit on the platform between the two criminals. I asked which province they came from, I asked about this and that, and then I got around to the preparations. But as I was in the middle of hearing their confession, I looked out the window and saw men carrying poles for the gallows and all that other stuff.

"'What's that?' the prisoners asked.

"'That,' I said to them, 'must be something they're building for the warden.'

"'No, reverend, that's for hanging us. What do you say, reverend, how about a little vodka?'

"'I don't know,' I said. 'I'll go find out.'

"I went to Colonel L and told him that the condemned wanted a drink. The Colonel gave me a bottle and instructed the jailer to remove the guard so there would be no talk. I got a glass from the sentry and went back to the prisoners in the cell. I filled a glass.

"'No, reverend,' they said. 'You first, or we won't drink.'

"I had to drink, but there wasn't anything to chase it down.

"'Well,' they said, 'vodka clears the head.'

"After this, I went on with the preparations. I talked with them for an hour and then another. Suddenly, the order:

"'Bring them out!'

"Afterwards, after they were hanged, I was afraid—from lack of experience—I was afraid to go into a dark room for a long, long time."

It is an early morning in October: gray, cold, and dark. The faces of the condemned have turned yellow from terror and the hair on their heads is quivering. The clerk trembles with agitation and stutters because he can barely see to read aloud the words of the death sentence. The priest, robed in a black cassock, holds up a crucifix to each of the nine men to kiss and then turns to the district commander, whispering,

"For God's sake, let me go, I cannot.... "

The procedure is long and involved. Each man must first be outfitted in a shroud before being led up to the gallows. When, at last, all nine have been hoisted up on their nooses, the group—as the district commander phrased it when giving me a description of the execution—looks like "a whole garland" hanging in the air. When the condemned were taken down from the gallows, the physicians discovered that one of them was still alive. This incident had a very special meaning: every member of the prison knows the secrets of all the crimes committed by every prisoner. In this case, the executioner and his assistants were aware that the survivor was in fact innocent of the crime for which he was executed.

"They hung him again." The district commander finished his story. "Afterwards, I was not able to sleep for a whole month."

## Juxtapose the Past and the Present

*When you give a description of a place, tell what it was like in the past and how it has changed, drawing on travelers' accounts and the reminiscences of old-time residents.*

One need only read Polyakov's account of Aleksandrovsk valley and compare it with what is there now, to appreciate how much heavy, truly punishing labor has gone into cultivating this area. "From the heights of neighboring mountains," writes Polyakov, "Aleksandrovsk valley appears overgrown, dark, and forested…a tremendous conifer forest covers a significant portion of the valley floor." He describes the swamps, the impenetrable quagmires, the repulsive soils and the forests where, "in addition to gigantic trees rising from bare roots, the ground is littered with monstrous, rotting logs felled by age or downed by winds; mossy hillocks poke out of the root balls of trees that have fallen across gullies and ravines." Now, however, instead of the taiga, the gullies, and the ravines, we find entire towns; streets have been laid out; meadows, fields of rye, and vegetable patches are green with new growth; and people are already complaining that the forests are disappearing.…

The Aleksandrovsk Post was established in 1881. An official who has been living on Sakhalin for the last ten years told me that when he first arrived at Aleksandrovsk Post, he nearly drowned in the mud. Father Irakly, who lived at Aleksandrovsk Post until 1886, told me that originally it had only three houses, and that the small barracks where the musicians now live used to house the prison. The streets were full of stumps. The brickworks now occupy what used to be a sable trapping area in 1882. Father Irakly was given the option of using the sentry booth as a church, but he turned it down because it was too small. Weather permitting, he would celebrate mass on the square; in bad weather he used the barracks or any other space that came available, and limited himself to officiating only at the morning service.

"There you are, celebrating mass, and all of a sudden chains start rattling," he told me. "It's noisy, the heat is infernal. I'm reciting, 'Holy, holy, holy…' while right next to me somebody's screaming, 'I'll break your g—— ....'" Every one of the various construction projects, including removing the stumps and draining the wetlands, was carried out by convicts. Until 1888, when the present prison was built, they were housed in yurts and dugouts, pits dug into the ground to a depth of four to five feet and covered with double-pitched sod roofs.... At present, Aleksandrovsk occupies an area of roughly 1.3 square miles.... Wooden sidewalks run along the streets. Everything is neat and tidy, and there are no puddles or heaps of rubbish even in alleys far from the center of town, in the poorest neighborhoods.

## Juxtapose the Unfamiliar with the Familiar

The northern part of Sakhalin Island—the area traversed by the permafrost belt—corresponds in its physical characteristics to Ryazan' province, and the south resembles the Crimea. The island is 594 miles in length; in width, it ranges from 82.5 miles across at its widest point, to 16.5 miles at the narrowest. The island is twice the size of Greece and one and a half times the size of Denmark.

When the zoologist Polyakov charted the Duyka River— also known as the Aleksandrovsk—he found it to be some seventy feet wide at its lower reaches. Enormous heaps of uprooted trees covered the banks. In many places, the lowlands were overgrown with old stands of fir, larch, alder, and willow, and surrounded by impassable bogs. Today the river resembles a long, narrow puddle. Its wide and bare banks and sluggish current make one think of the Moscow Canal.

At first glance, Korsakov looks deceptively like one of those charming, backward, typically Russian villages that are still untouched by civilization. On my first visit, I arrived on a Sunday, after dinner. The weather was calm, warm, and there was a festive feel in the air. Peasants were napping in the shade or drinking tea. Women were sitting outside the huts, by the doors or under the windows, and picking lice out of each other's hair. There were flowers in the small yards and gardens, and the sills of the windows were filled with geraniums. The street was full of children playing at soldiers or trying to ride "horsy" on fat dogs who would rather have been sleeping.

## Decide What Names to Use

*Identify the characters by first and last name, and when in doubt, use initials.*

The following day I paid a visit to the commandant of the island, V. O. Kononovich. Though fatigued and short of time, the general received me most graciously and spent about an hour conversing with me.

"Allow me to introduce myself," the official said. " I am Collegiate Registrar D."

This was my first Sakhalin acquaintance, a poet, the author of a mock epic entitled *Sakhalinó*, which began with the words: "Tell me, doctor, in vain was it that...." Subsequently he became a frequent visitor and walking companion around Aleksandrovsk and its surroundings, regaling me with anecdotes and endless recitations of his own poetry. On long winter evenings he writes stories with a liberal cast, but if necessary is quick to remind people that he is a Collegiate Registrar, Tenth Class.[11] Once, when a peasant woman came to see him on business and addressed him as "Mister D," he took offense and furiously corrected her: "I am no 'Mister D' to you: I am 'Your Worship!'"

## Provide Summaries of Chapters

*It might be useful to begin each chapter with a detailed summary of the central arguments.*

Chapter III. The Census. Contents of the Statistical Forms. The Questions I Posed and the Answers I Received. Peasant Homes and Their Occupants. Exiles' Opinions of the Census.

Chapter XXII. Sakhalin Escapees. Reasons for Escape. Breakdown of Escapees by Origin, Rank, Etc.

# LAST THINGS

## Where to Publish

*Letter to Alexei Suvorin, January 2, 1894*

My *Sakhalin* is an academic work and will win me the Metropolitan Macarius Award.[12] Medicine will no longer be able to reproach me with disloyalty: I will have paid my dues to scholarship and to what the old writers used to call pedantry. And I am pleased to add this convict coat to the closet of my literary wardrobe. Let it hang there! I should not, of course, try to publish *Sakhalin* in the...[*New Times*] since this is not a journalistic piece. But I do think that a small, separate volume could be useful.

## Plan Your Celebration

*Letter to Yakov Korneyev,* [13] *March 27, 1894*

Most honorable Yakov Alekseevich! I had a plan: to bring you a copy of my *Sakhalin*—with an appropriate inscription—as soon as it appeared in print. But as I was about to take a cab to the railway station, that is, at the very beginning of my journey, you forced me to drink three glasses of Santorini wine "for the road," and those three glasses, as much as your good wishes, evidently served me well, because I traveled safely.

## Plan Your Next Trip

*Letter to Alexei Suvorin, July 11, 1894*

This is my plan. On July 20 or 22, I will go to Taganrog to tend my uncle who is seriously ill and insists on my treating him. He is an excellent man, and it would be awkward to refuse, although I am certain that my help will do him no good. I will be spending between one and three days in Taganrog, swimming in the sea, visiting the cemetery—and then, back to Moscow. Now that I am done with *Sakhalin* and have given my thanks to the powers above, I proclaim myself a free man, ready to go wherever I please.

# ACKNOWLEDGMENTS

Matthew Lore, my esteemed editor, for your vision, patience, friendship, and chocolate cake.

Collin Tracy and Cynthia Buck, for your rapid assessment and response.

Jeff Goebel, for never letting me forget.

Anya Yatsenko, for your erudite answers to my questions.

Peter Steinberger, for your stalwart support.

Gideon and Tanya Bosker, for your patient hospitality.

Bianca Oona Lenček Bosker, for your laughter, curiosity, and example.

Nina Antonia Hedviga Lovrenčič Lenček, for being my best reader. Ever.

# WHO'S WHO IN
# CHEKHOV'S CORRESPONDENCE
❧

THE NUMBER AND RANGE OF CONTEMPORARIES WHO
appear in Chekhov's correspondence, either as interlocu-
tors or as subject matter, are staggering. This skeletal guide,
in alphabetical order, is intended as the briefest of introduc-
tions to readers curious about those of Chekhov's literary
and social connections who appear in this book.

**Avilova, Lydia Alexandrovna (1864–1942).** A writer and
memoirist, Avilova was a devoted admirer of Chekhov who
entertained hopes—and, it seems, delusions—of a close relationship, despite her marriage and motherhood. After the
writer's death, she published an account of their friendship
in which she detailed all eight of their encounters between
1889 and 1899. Chekhov himself shed no light on the matter,
leaving a field ripe for speculation that continues to engage
scholars.

**Batyushkov, Fyodor Dmitrievich (1857–1920).** A distinguished literary scholar, a founder of Russian study of

comparative literature, and editor of the Russian section of the international journal *Cosmopolis*.

**Burenin, Viktor Petrovich (1841–1926).** A critic and playwright and, for a time, an editor of *New Times* (*Novoye Vremya*), to which Chekhov contributed many stories. Highly reactionary and known for his cynicism and bad manners in print, Burenin nonetheless gave Chekhov's "The Steppe" a favorable review.

**Chekhov, Alexander Pavlovich (1855–1913).** Anton's oldest brother, who launched the family business of writing and publishing for money. A contributor to *New Times*, Alexander was plagued by alcoholism, common-law marriages, and a bitter disposition.

**Chekhov, Mikhail Pavlovich (Misha) (1865–1936).** The youngest of the Chekhov sons, Mikhail followed in his brother's footsteps by dividing his professional loyalties between the law and literature. Writing under several pseudonyms, including M. Bogemnsky, M. B-sky, M. Ch., Maksim Kholyava, and Kaptan Kuk, he was the author of stories, children's stories, plays, essays, reviews, and humorous sketches; he also published a magazine and left valuable reminiscences of his brother.

**Chekhova, Maria Pavlovna (Masha) (1864–1957).** Anton's only sister, Maria idolized her brother, never married, and both during and after his lifetime dedicated herself to his work. She published the first six-volume edition of her brother's letters between 1912 and 1916 and maintained his villa in Yalta as a museum.

**Gilyarovsky, Vladimir Alekseyevich (1853–1935).** A flamboyant adventurer, crime journalist, writer, circus performer, and friend of Chekhov's whose literary niche was the messy underbelly of Moscow life. His portrait appears among the faces of the Cossacks in Ilya Repin's monumental painting *The Reply of the Zaporozhian Cossacks* (1880–91).

**Gorky, Maxim, pseudonym of Alexei Maksimovich Peshkov (1868–1936).** The originator of socialist realism, the official aesthetic of the Soviet Union. Endowed with a generous and charismatic personality, the writer, playwright, poet, critic, and literary entrepreneur did much to preserve the lives of fellow writers and the humanist values of prerevolutionary culture during the early years of the Revolution. As a young orphan, Gorky had survived by odd jobs; he became fearless and developed radical political views. His friendships with Chekhov and Tolstoy helped cement his commitment to literature and advanced his standing among his contemporaries. His perceptive and fond reminiscences of Chekhov make for excellent reading.

**Grigorovich, Dmitry Vasilevich (1822–99).** One of the key literary figures of the second half of the nineteenth century, Grigorovich built his reputation chiefly on a number of short stories about peasant life he wrote in the 1840s as a member of the so-called Natural School. His most lasting contribution to literature, however, derives from his sponsorship of two of Russia's greatest writers: Fyodor Dostoevsky, his roommate in 1844, whom he brought to the attention of the poet-publisher Nekrasov and the critic Belinsky; and Anton Chekhov, whom, in a letter in 1886, he hailed as the most outstanding writer of the young generation. Grigorovich's encouragement has been regarded as instrumental in transforming the hack "Antosha Chekhonte" into the serious writer Anton Chekhov. Chekhov's letters to the older writer were models of filial respect, though their relations had cooled by 1889 with Grigorovich's tepid response to Chekhov's experiments in the theater.

**Khotyaintseva, Alexandra Alexandrovna (1865–1942).** A talented artist who struck up an acquaintance with Chekhov through his sister Masha, whose portrait she painted in Melikhovo. Chekhov especially appreciated her sensitive renderings of the landscape and called her "a great artist of the Russian land." Khotyaintseva cherished a portfolio of caricatures dating from her sojourn in Nice, where Chekhov was seeking a cure for tuberculosis, which she called the *Chekhiad.*

**Kiselyova, Maria Vladimirovna (1857–1923).** A successful writer of children's stories, a passionate angler, and granddaughter of the eighteenth-century writer and publisher N. I. Novikov. She befriended Chekhov in the countryside in Ukraine when the Chekhov family leased a nearby villa. The Kiselyovs owned the elegant Babkino estate, where

Chekhov was a frequent and welcome guest and came into contact with a constant stream of visiting writers and musicians. Maria was the first of a number of women writers— among them Elena Shavrova and Lydia Avilova—whom he mentored. Chekhov's sister jokingly referred to the bevy of Chekhov's female admirers as the "Antonovkas," a charming play on the name of the fragrant apple cultivar beloved of dacha owners in prerevolutionary Russia.

**Knipper, Olga Leonardovna (1869–1959).** A member of the Moscow Art Theater, founded by V. I. Nemirovich-Danchenko and Konstantin Stanislavsky, Knipper performed in all the original productions of Chekhov's plays at the Moscow Art Theater. The author first saw her on stage in 1898, as the Empress Irina in the premiere of A. K. Tolstoy's *Czar Fyodor Ioannovich*. Of his first impression of the woman who would become his wife Chekhov wrote: "[She] is magnificent. Her voice, nobility, sincerity—are so fine that they make my throat tickle.... If I were to stay in Moscow, I would certainly fall in love with this Irina." They were married in 1901. The object of much envy and gossip, Olga provoked dismay by remaining in Moscow and continuing to devote herself to the theater while Chekhov was ailing, alone, in Yalta. The love letters, collected, translated, and published by Constance Garnett in 1926, attest to a passionate friendship.

**Korneyev, Yakov Alekseevich (no date).** A genial physician whose role in Chekhov's life was largely confined to owning the building on Sadovaya-Kudrinskaya Street in Moscow where the Chekhov family resided between 1886 and 1890. The two-story apartment in which five members of the Chekhov family lived was located in a wing that resembled a small castle. Chekhov's study and bedroom were on the main floor.

**Korolenko, Vladimir Galaktionovich (1853–1921).** A novelist and left-wing liberal who took a politically engaged position in life and in art, championing the rights of peasants, decrying anti-Semitism, and joining with Chekhov in protesting the exclusion of Gorky from the Academy of Sciences by resigning their own titles as Honorary Academicians in 1902. Korolenko's "Sakhalin Fugitive" may have inspired Chekhov's interest in writing about the penal colony.

**Lavrov, Vukol Mikhailovich (1852–1912).** Scion of a wealthy Moscow merchant family, Lavrov was the owner, publisher, and editor of the left-liberal literary journal *Russian Thought* (*Russkaya Mysl'*). He distinguished himself as a journalist and as a translator of Polish writers (most notably Henryk Stankiewicz) and hosted extravagant literary dinner parties.

**Lazarev-Gruzinsky, Alexander (1861–1927).** Under the pen name A. Gruzinsky, wrote in the humor magazine in which Chekhov began his literary career. He met Chekhov in 1887 at the magazine's editorial offices, though by this point

Chekhov had already "graduated" to more prestigious venues. With Chekhov's help and mentoring, he gained entrée to *New Times* and other major journals and publications.

**Leontyev (Shcheglov), Ivan (1856–1911).** A writer for the theater. In his diary entry for December 9, 1888, he wrote that Chekhov lacked moral principles and "a general animating idea." On February 9, 1889, he noted that an acquaintance had said, "Chekhov is a genius, but does not have God in his soul."

**Leykin, Nikolai Alexandrovich (1841–1906).** Publisher of the St. Petersburg humor magazine *Fragments* (*Oskolki*), to which Chekhov contributed stories between 1883 and 1885. Leykin was a great promoter of the Chekhov brothers, helping them with money and publishing opportunities in his magazine and publishing firm. He liked to claim that he first "discovered" Anton Chekhov. He himself also wrote novels and stories about the Russian merchant class.

**Menshikov, Mikhail Osipovich (1859–1917).** A prominent journalist, editor of the St. Petersburg magazine *The Week* (*Nedelya*), and contributor to Alexei Suvorin's *New Times* (*Novoye Vremya*) between 1901 and 1917.

**Mikhailovsky, Nikolai Konstantinovich (1842–1904).** An influential literary critic and editor of the "thick journals" *Notes of the Fatherland* (*Otechestvennye Zapiski*) and *Russian Wealth* (*Russkoe Bogatstvo*). As the leading theoretician of populism, he required of literature a pronounced social, political, and moral agenda.

**Orlov, Ivan Ivanovich (1851–1917).** A surgeon who practiced in a district adjoining the Serpukhov zemstvo where Chekhov practiced during his stay at Melikhovo. The two physicians frequently corresponded on matters bearing on the organization of health care in the countryside and the state of the intelligentsia.

**Pleshcheyev, Alexei Nikolayevich (1825–93).** Poet, essayist, translator, and, in his youth, a principled liberal who was exiled to Siberia. Pleshcheyev was the editor of the *Northern Herald* (*Severnii Vestnik*), in which he published Chekhov's stories between 1887 and 1889. The two enjoyed a close friendship, with Pleshcheyev visiting Chekhov during summer holidays in the country.

**Polonsky, Yakov Petrovich (1819–98).** One of Russia's leading poets during the poetic doldrums following the death of Alexander Sergeyevich Pushkin in 1837. Chekhov and Polonsky respected each other's work, and each dedicated a work to the other.

**Rossolimo, Grigory Ivanovich (1860–1928).** Of Greek origin, Rossolimo studied with Chekhov at the Moscow University Medical School, whose faculty he subsequently joined as a specialist in neurology and psychology. A dynamic clinician, researcher, and scholar, Rossolimo kept in steady contact with Chekhov and was especially attentive and solicitous in the final years of Chekhov's precipitous decline.

**Shavrova, Elena Mikhailovna (1874–1937).** One of a group of Maria Chekhova's girlfriends and schoolmates with whom Chekhov carried on light flirtations. The Chekhov home was always filled with friends and associates, lively conversation, serious debate, and, unfailingly, laughter. Fifteen when she met Chekhov, Elena went on, with his help, to have a modest literary success.

**Suvorin, Alexei Sergeyevich (1834–1912).** One of the most powerful and influential "men of letters" of nineteenth-century Russia. A peasant by origin and a schoolmaster by training, Suvorin entered the literary profession in the 1860s and rose to prominence first as a muckraking journalist, then as owner and publisher of the conservative *New Times*, which he took over in 1876. He was also involved with all the leading journals of the age, including *Russian Speech (Russkaya Rech')*, *The Contemporary (Sovremennik)*, *Notes of the Fatherland (Otechestvennye Zapiski)*, and *Herald of Europe (Vestnik Evropy)*. The "media empire" of this literary entrepreneur included a chain of his own bookstores in Russia's major cities where his editions of Russian and translated writers were sold. Novelist, literary scholar, and playwright, he wrote fiction under the pseudonyms Bobrovsky and Neznakomets, and in what was characterized as "tragic handwriting," his extensive *Diary*, a valuable source of information on the literary and historical events of his time. Suvorin made a fortune as a renaissance man of letters and was a great admirer, patron, and friend of Chekhov.

**Tchaikovsky, Modest Ilyich (1850–1916).** Playwright, librettist, translator of Shakespeare, and younger brother of the composer Peter Ilyich Tchaikovsky. Chekhov, a great devotee of the composer, met Modest in St. Petersburg in 1888 at the home of the poet Pleshcheyev. The acquaintance led to meetings with the composer, who stunned Chekhov by recognizing him as a rising talent. Chekhov dedicated a volume of his stories to Peter, who reciprocated by sending him a signed photograph with the inscription "To A. P. Chekhov from his ardent admirer. P. Tchaikovsky, October 14, 1889."

**Tikhonov, Vladimir Alekseyevich (1857–1914).** A minor playwright and briefly editor of the magazine *North* (*Sever*). Tikhonov was a loyal supporter of Chekhov, who enjoyed his company and correspondence for a number of years.

**Yegorov, Yevgraf Petrovich (no date).** After Yegorov became a friend of the Chekhov family in 1883–84, while stationed in the military at Voskresensk, it appears that he fell in love with Maria Chekhova and proposed. After leaving the army in 1891, he settled in Nizhny Novgorod province, where he served as a humane and enlightened local land captain overseeing judicial and administrative peasant affairs. Chekhov modeled a character on Yegorov in his story "Green Braid"("Zelyonaya kosa") from that period.

**Evreinova, Anna Mikhailovna (1844–1919).** The first Russian woman to receive a doctorate in law. Evreinova attained a position of cultural influence as the publisher of the *Northern Herald*, in which Chekhov published a great many of his stories.

**Zhirkevich, Alexander Vladimirovich (1875–1927).** A minor poet, writer (under the pseudonym A. Nivin), and essayist with a prominent career in military jurisprudence. Highly cultivated, a passionate collector of manuscripts, drawings, medieval instruments of torture, and prominent artists and writers, he carried on extensive correspondence with Leskov, Fet, Sologub, and Chekhov and was an occasional visitor at Leo Tolstoy's Yasnaya Polyana. Like Vladimir Gilyarovsky, he appears in Ilya Repin's *The Reply of the Zaporozhian Cossacks* (1880–91).

# AFTERWORD
# BY PIERO BRUNELLO

❧

*Translated by Lena Lenček*

## A Life in Brief

The century was coming to an end, and Chekhov—at the age of thirty-nine still morbidly averse to writing about himself—complied with a request for a publishable auto-biography by scribbling the following account:

> I, A. P. Chekhov, was born on January 17, 1860, in Taganrog. I was educated first at the Greek School of the Church of the Emperor Constantine, and then at the Taganrog gymnasium. In 1879, I enrolled in the medical school of Moscow University. I had a rather vague idea of the university at the time, and now cannot recall exactly what made me settle on medical school, but I have subse-quently not come to regret my choice. During my first year, I began publishing in weekly magazines and news-papers, and by the early '80s, these literary activities had taken on a permanent, professional character. In 1888, I was awarded the Pushkin Prize. In 1890, I traveled to the Island of Sakhalin with the intention of later writing a

book about our colony of exiles and penal servitude. Not counting trial reports, reviews, feuilletons, news reports, and the columns I wrote for the daily press and that would be difficult to locate and collect, I have written over forty-eight hundred pages of novellas and stories during the twenty years I have been active in literature. I have also written plays for the theater.

I've no doubt that my work in medicine has had a serious impact on my literary work; it has significantly broadened the scope of my observations, and has enriched me with knowledge whose true value for me as a writer can be appreciated only by another physician. It also had a decisive guiding influence: my intimacy with medicine helped me avoid many mistakes. My familiarity with the natural sciences and with the scientific method always kept me on my guard; I have endeavored, whenever possible, to take scientific facts into account, and where this was not possible, I preferred to not write at all. I might note, by the way, that the conditions of creative art do not always permit full concord with scientific facts; death by poison cannot be represented on the stage as it actually occurs in life. However, some conformity with scientific data must be perceptible even within the bounds of artistic convention; in other words, the reader or spectator should be able to sense clearly that there is a convention at work, and that the author is knowledgeable about the situation at hand.

I do not count myself among those writers who have a negative attitude toward medicine; nor would I wish to be one of those who want to figure out everything for themselves.

As for my medical practice, as a student I worked in the Voskresensk Zemstvo Hospital (near the New

Jerusalem Monastery) under the eminent zemstvo doctor Pavel A. Arkhangelsky, and went on to do a short tour as a doctor in the Zvenigorod Hospital. During the years of the cholera epidemic (1892 and 1893), I was in charge of the Melikhovo region of the Serpukhov district.[1]

Typical of Chekhov is the way he juggles the two professions—writing and medicine—between which he divided his energies. Equally typical is his silence on the subject of his own illness. An acute attack of peritonitis at the age of fifteen left him with chronic digestive problems. The first symptoms of tuberculosis appeared nine years later. He managed to ignore them until the age of thirty-seven, when it was no longer possible to do so. The turning point came one evening in a fashionable Moscow restaurant when suddenly, over dinner with his publisher, editor, and friend Alexei Suvorin, "without warning, blood began gushing from his mouth." Raymond Carver re-creates the scene in a story dedicated to the author. "Suvorin and two waiters helped him to the gentlemen's room and tried to stanch the flow of blood with icepacks." They rushed him to a clinic. "When Suvorin visited him there, Chekhov apologized for the 'scandal' at the restaurant three nights earlier but continued to insist there was nothing seriously wrong. 'He laughed and jested as usual,' Suvorin noted in his diary, 'while spitting blood into a large vessel.'"[2]

The recovery was temporary, followed by longer and longer "cures" on the French Riviera, the Crimea, and, finally, in a sanatorium at Badenweiler in the Black Forest. With him was the actress Olga Knipper, whom he had married three years earlier. One night he asked her to summon a physician. He had never done this before. Olga instantly complied and called for ice, which, with the help of a Russian student lodging in the hotel, she began to crush and scatter on the floor.

"Doctor Schwörer," Olga writes in her diary, "arrived and began to speak gently, cradling Anton Pavlovich in his arms. Chekhov sat up and in a loud, strong voice said to the doctor, 'Ich sterbe.'[3] The doctor tried to calm him, gave him a camphor injection, and ordered a bottle of champagne. Anton Pavlovich picked up the full glass, studied it closely, smiled at me, and said: 'It's been such a long time since I've had champagne.' He drank it all to the last drop, quietly stretched out on his left side; I had just managed to run to him and bend over him in the bed, and call to him, but he had already stopped breathing; he had fallen asleep, like a child. ... And when that which had been Anton Pavlovich had left, a huge, gray nocturnal moth came in through the window and kept crashing painfully into the walls, the ceiling, the lamps as though in his death throes."[4]

Chekhov died on July 2, 1904. He was forty-four years old.

## The Sakhalin Project

In 1890 Chekhov set off on a journey to Sakhalin, a remote island in the Sea of Okhotsk that was colonized largely by convicts and political exiles. Chekhov's friends and family were aghast at his decision to embark on such an arduous adventure, all the more so because he was beginning to show symptoms of the same galloping consumption that a year earlier had killed his brother Nikolai at the age of thirty. What could posses Anton to make such a journey?

Chekhov gave several reasons. He wanted to gather information about deportation[5]; he needed a change from the routine[6]; he wanted to write a doctoral dissertation in medicine.[7] He fantasized about navigating rivers by steamboat and crossing the steppes in horse-drawn carriages.[8] He wanted to emulate two of his favorite heroes, the Russian explorer Nikolai Przhevalsky, who had ventured into Central Asia and had wanted to be buried in the desert; and the American journalist Henry Stanley, who had tracked down the missionary-explorer David Livingstone in the depths of Africa. These men inspired him because they had done something significant with their lives.[9] In a letter to twenty-year-old Natalya Lintvaryova, he playfully asked whether she would preserve his memory should he be mauled by bears or murdered by vagabonds, two of the many hazards associated with travel in Siberia.[10]

His true motive, however, appears to have sprung from moral outrage with a barbaric system of justice that "sent *millions* to rot in prisons" and "drove people in chains, thousands of miles through the cold, infected them with syphilis, turned them into degenerates, [and] bred criminals."[11] Chekhov believed that "each one of us" had to bear responsibility for such appalling conditions, no matter how remote and distant they might be from people's lives. For him, writing about Sakhalin would be a way to fight indifference. Although a number of books had been written about Sakhalin, not one of them, in his opinion, rose above the level of rhetorical exercises. "Generally speaking," he wrote to Suvorin, "in our beloved homeland there is a great poverty of facts and a great wealth of the most diverse rationalizations: the more books I read about Sakhalin, the more convinced I am that this...is a place of the most unbearable suffering of which man is capable."[12]

Chekhov drew up a research program. He began with travelogues, one of his favorite genres. He loved reading about Charles Darwin's global expedition. Since childhood, he had been entranced by Ivan Goncharov's *The Frigate Pallada* (1858), an account of the author's journey from St. Petersburg by way of the Atlantic and Indian Oceans to Ceylon, Japan, and the eastern coast of Russia, and thence, overland, across Siberia. Chekhov drew up a bibliography of everything he could find on the subject of Sakhalin: the journals of explorers, geographical tracts, and investigations into the zoology, botany, ethnography, mineralogy, geology, and meteorology of the island. He collected books, articles, and statistics on the Russian penal system. From Alexei Suvorin he obtained maps, atlases, and publications that were beyond his reach or means. He prevailed on his sister Masha and a young woman friend to make copies of journals in the Moscow library, and he persuaded his brother Alexander to do the same in St. Petersburg. From an actress named Kleopatra Karatygina, who had spent many years in Siberia, he obtained a list of contacts and practical advice, including the suggestion that he never ask anyone the reason why they had been brought to Siberia. His letters spoke of nothing but Sakhalin, and all his time went into research. In jest, he diagnosed himself as afflicted with *Mania Sakhalinosa.*[13]

Friends advised him to secure official letters of introduction to the Sakhalin administrators. Chekhov refused: he saw no point in applying to authorities who had a vested interest in maintaining public indifference to the plight of prisoners and exiles. In January 1890, however, he did obtain authorization to conduct literary and scientific research on the island from Mikhail N. Galkin-Vraskoy, the head of the national prison administration.[14] Fearful of what Chekhov might uncover, Galkin-Vraskoy secretly directed island authorities to bar the writer from contact with political prisoners and stipulated that any findings be submitted for approval before publication in Suvorin's paper.[15]

It took Chekhov ten weeks to cover the roughly 7,500 miles by land across Siberia. He traveled by train, steamer, and tarantass ("a sort of wicker basket") drawn by two horses, with a change of private drivers at each village station. Bumping across the steppe and slogging through mud, Chekhov felt as if his stomach were coming out of his mouth: he was exhausted in every part of his body, and his feet seemed to be turning to ice. Nevertheless, he scrupulously scribbled his impressions in pencil and sent them to his editor and his family. His letters from the road are filled with detailed descriptions of the landscape, the people, the discomforts of the road, and humorous insights. Finally, on July 5, 1890, Chekhov arrived in Nikolayevsk.[16]

On the island itself, he traveled by train, cart, carriage, and steamboat. The fieldwork was exhausting. "I've gone around to each of the settlements," he wrote, "stopped at each hut, and talked with each person. For purposes of the census, I made use of a file card system and have already compiled records of around ten thousand convicts and settlers. In other words, there is not a single convict or settler left on Sakhalin who has not talked with me." He "visited all the celebrities" of the island.[17] He turned down offers of assistance, preferring to conduct his census alone. He was not interested in the numerical part of the census, but in meetings with people and what he saw and experienced within himself in the course of his research.

Chekhov visited homes, kitchens, prisons, workshops, latrines, clinics, hospitals, villages, barracks, churches, farms, cemeteries, schools, and mines. He made inquiries about the status of agriculture and fishing and studied the climate, soil, water, and condition of the forests. He examined police registries and reports and interviewed inmates, soldiers, officials, administrators, guards, exiles, and priests. He made ethnographic observations on the Ghiliaks and the Ainu and concluded that "Russification" attempts had had a negative impact on their lives and morale. He looked into the medical condition of children, discovered that women were treated no better than animals, and learned that young girls were forced into prostitution. He railed against the particular medical condition afflicting the islanders, which he called "*febris sakhaliniensis*"; he attributed it to the brutal labor regimen, the harsh climate, the appalling rations, the stress, and the physical and psychological abuse.

By the time he was ready to leave, Chekhov had collected 7,500 index cards, an assortment of souvenirs given to him by convicts, a notebook, the island commandant's orders of the day, a sheaf of petitions, and personal letters. An outbreak of cholera forced him to return by way of the Sea of Japan, the Indian Ocean, Ceylon, and the Suez Canal. Once home, he felt like a trunk stuffed full of documents and proceeded to draft his report. The writing, however, was difficult and proceeded by fits and starts. One problem was the necessity of getting the work past the censor; another was securing the approval of Mikhail Galkin-Vraskoy, the chief administrator of all the prisons and penal institutions of the Russian Empire.

Chekhov dashed off a sketch on escapes from Sakhalin, which would become one of the final chapters, and published it in December 1891 in a publication to benefit famine victims. Then the writing faltered. In the summer of 1892, Chekhov wrote to Suvorin that he could not write as long as "a Galkin-Vraskoy rules the prisons."[18] In fact, however, he could not quite find the right tone: to his ear, everything he wrote had a false ring. Eventually, he figured out the problem. "The insincere quality," he wrote to Suvorin, "stemmed from the sense that I was trying to make *Sakhalin* instructive even as I was concealing something and holding myself back. But as soon as I realized how much I had felt myself to be an eccentric on Sakhalin and what swine there were on that island, I felt relieved and my writing took off, though it turned out a touch humorous."[19]

The final version of the text, which appeared three years after the journey to Sakhalin, betrays Chekhov's fear of the censor. There is nothing even remotely tendentious or anything that might suggest he is passing judgment. Chekhov scrupulously confines himself to facts. Wherever possible, he replaces the first-person pronoun with impersonal expressions: "I think" becomes "one might say." Chekhov's name never appears in the text. Nor does he refer to himself as a physician except in the last chapter, in which he describes a surgical procedure that he performed. Instead, the impersonal narrator stands for Chekhov the traveler, whose persona gives the impression of someone who is ready to believe everything he hears, goes on picnics, and fights boredom with fishing. The author's personality vanishes. He emerges here in the guise of an everyman who observes honestly and without prejudice and tells what he sees. He is neither an omniscient guide nor a curious tourist, nor—least of all—a prophet.[20]

## The Lessons of Sakhalin

The Sakhalin project helped Chekhov understand why he wrote and prompted him to reflect on the goals of his writing. He learned that "life is a march to prison. Literature should genuinely teach either how one can escape or it should promise freedom."[21] He also gained insights into the particular quality of life in his native land. "Life in Russia crushes the Russian until there's nothing left, not even a wet spot; it crushes like a twenty-ton rock."[22] He admitted now that he felt out of place in his own land and understood that writing represented an act of freedom in a country "where there was no freedom of press or freedom of conscience …where life was so narrow and foul and there was so little hope for better times."[23] Nevertheless, he did not want to preach; rather, he wanted to be "a mere chronicler… [of] the unconditional and honest truth."[24]

Chekhov never belonged to any political movement. He was not the type, according to Vladimir Nabokov, because he "believed that the first thing needed was justice, and all his life he raised his voice against every kind of injustice; but he did it as a writer. Chekhov was in the first place an individualist and an artist."[25] Nabokov's observation helps explain why Chekhov's advice on writing is at the same time advice on living. Chekhov insists on "painting life as it is" and not "lying to oneself." Truth and honesty are at the very basis of good writing, because they are the basis of personal behavior and political action. No "radiant future," no "love for the future," can justify falsehood, as Chekhov wrote in a letter to his editor Suvorin.[26]

Chekhov's response to the Dreyfus Affair of 1894 epitomizes this moral integrity. He found that events in France had taken "an ugly turn toward the terrain of anti-Semitism, a terrain that stinks of slaughter." He admired Émile Zola because the French naturalist based his judgment only "on what he sees, and not, like others, on phantoms." Chekhov believed that when something inside us is amiss, "we seek the causes outside ourselves and before long we find them: it's the French who are making a mess, it's the Yids, it's Wilhelm. . . . Capitalism, the bogeyman, the Masons, the syndicate, the Jesuits—they may be nothing but phantoms, but do they ever lighten our troubled conscience!" As far as Chekhov was concerned, even if Alfred Dreyfus had been guilty and Zola had been in error, their culpability would still be less dangerous, because stemming from sincerity, than actions prompted by "deliberate insincerity, prejudice, or political considerations."[27]

Chekhov did not believe in the moral authority of intellectuals, political parties, the press, or the intelligentsia as a whole. He did have faith in individuals. "I see salvation in individuals scattered here and there, all over Russia, be they intellectuals or peasants makes no difference, for the real power is in them, no matter how few there may be. No man is a prophet in his own land; and the individuals of whom I speak play an imperceptible role in their society. They are not dominant, but their work is visible."[28]

The individual he admired exercised freedom, whatever the price. When Chekhov's brother Alexander began publishing, the author gave him the following counsel: "By saying, 'I don't like this!' you have already affirmed your independence and even utility."[29] He saw no need for the "private, professional, clubby solidarity" of intellectuals. Instead, he admired the free, unallied intellectual. In a statement that has since been taken as his profession of faith, Chekhov proclaimed, "I look upon labels and tags as prejudices. My holy of holies is the human body, health, intelligence, inspiration, love, and the most absolute freedom—freedom from violence and falsehood, whatever forms the latter two might take. This is the program to which I would adhere were I a great artist."[30]

# FOR FURTHER READING

✥

The reader may wish to explore the following sources:

## Chekhov's Letters

Chekhov, Anton. *A Life in Letters*. Edited by Rosamund Bartlett. Translated by Rosamund Bartlett and Anthony Phillips (New York: Penguin, 2004).

Chekhov, Anton. *Letters of Anton Chekhov to His Family and Friends with Biographical Sketch*. Edited by Constance Garnett (New York: Macmillan, 1920). Available through the Project Guttenberg Literary Archive Foundation at: http://www.gutenberg.net/etext/6408.

Chekhov, Anton, and Olga Knipper. *The Love Letters of Anton Chekhov and Olga Knipper*. Edited and translated by Jean Benedetti (London: Methuen, 2007).

Friedland, Louis, editor and translator. *Letters on the Short Story, the Drama, and Other Literary Topics by Anton Chekhov* (New York: B. Blom, 1964).

Garnett, Constance, editor and translator. *The Letters of Anton Pavlovitch Tchehov to Olga Leonardovna Knipper* (London: Chatto & Windus, 1926).

Hellman, Lillian, editor and introduction. *The Selected Letters of Anton Chekhov*. Translated by Sidonie K. Lederer (New York: Farrar, Straus & Giroux, 1984).

Karlinsky, Simon, editor and introduction. *Anton Chekhov's Life and Thought: Selected Letters and Commentary*. Translated by Michael Henry Heim and Simon Karlinsky (New York: Harper & Row, 1973).

Koteliansky, S. S., and Philip Tomlinson, editors and translators. *The Life and Letters of Anton Tchekhov* (New York: George H. Doran, 1925).

McVay, Gordon, editor and translator. *Chekhov: A Life in Letters* (London: Folio Society, 1994).

Yarmolinsky, Avrahm, selector and editor. *Letters of Anton Chekhov* (New York: Harper & Row, 1973).

## About Chekhov

Callow, Philip. *Chekhov, The Hidden Ground: A Biography* (Chicago: Ivan R. Dee, 1998).

Chukovsky, Kornej. *Chekhov: The Man* (New York: Hutchinson, 1945).

Clayton, J. Douglas, editor. *Chekhov Then and Now: The Reception of Chekhov in World Culture* (New York: Peter Lang, 1997).

Gerhardie, William A. *Anton Chekhov: A Critical Study* (London: Duckworth, 1928).

Gorky, Maxim. *Reminiscences of Tolstoy, Chekhov, and Andreyev* (New York: Farrar, Straus, 1955).

Jackson, Robert Louis, editor. *Chekhov: A Collection of Critical Essays* (Englewood Cliffs, N.J.: Prentice-Hall, 1967).

Maegd-Soëp, Carolina de. *Chekhov and Women: Women in the Life and Work of Chekhov* (Columbus, Ohio: Slavica, 1987).

Magarshack, David. *Chekhov: A Life* (New York: Grove Press, 1953).

Matlaw, Ralph E. *Anton Chekhov's Short Stories: Texts of the Stories, Backgrounds, Criticism* (New York: Norton, 1979).

Pritchett, V. S. *Chekhov: A Spirit Set Free* (New York: Random House, 1988).

Rayfield, Donald. *Anton Chekhov: A Life* (New York: Henry Holt, 1998).

Simmons, Ernest J. *Chekhov: A Biography* (Boston: Little, Brown, 1962).

Toumanova, Nina A. *Chekhov: The Voice of Twilight Russia* (New York: Columbia University Press, 1937).

Troyat, Henri. *Chekhov* (New York: Dutton, 1986).

Winner, Thomas. *Chekhov and His Prose* (New York: Holt, Rinehart and Winston, 1966).

Yarmolinsky, Avrahm, translator and introduction. *The Unknown Chekhov: Stories and Other Writings* (New York: Minerva Press, 1954).

## Cultural Background

Billington, James A. *The Icon and the Axe: An Interpretive History of Russian Culture* (New York: Vintage Books, 1970).

Figes, Orlando. *Natasha's Dance: A Cultural History of Russia* (New York: Henry Holt, 2002).

Hosking, Geoffrey. *Russia and the Russians: A History* (Cambridge, Mass.: Harvard University Press, 2001).

Rzhevsky, Nicholas, editor. *The Cambridge Companion to Modern Russian Culture* (Cambridge: Cambridge University Press, 1998).

# NOTES

## Preface and Introduction

1. Anton Cechov, *Senza trame e senza finale: 99 consigli di scrittura*, ed. Piero Brunello, trans. Gigliola Venturi and Clara Coïsson (Rome: Minimum Fax, 2002); Anton Cechov, *Scarpe buone e un quaderno di appunti: Come fare un reportage*, ed. Piero Brunello, trans. Nadia Caprioglio and Giovanna Spendel (Rome: Minimum Fax, 2004).

2. A. P. Chekhov, *Ostrov Sakhalin: (Iz putevykh zapisok) Polnoe sobranie sochinenii i pisem, Sochineniia*, vols. 14–15 (Moscow: Izdatel'stvo "Nauka," 1978). In English, the title is generally given as *The Island of Sakhalin*. Chekhov spent four years on his Sakhalin project. After extensive preliminary research in St. Petersburg and Moscow, he set off for the czarist penal colony on April 21, 1890, and returned on December 9 of the same year. He was on Sakhalin from July 11 through October 30. He published his *Sakhalin Island: Travel Notes* in 1895. [L.L.]

3. Raymond Carver, *No Heroics, Please: Uncollected Writings* (New York: Vintage, 1992), and *What We Talk About When We Talk About Love: Stories* (New York: Vintage, 1989).

4. Claude Bernard, *An Introduction to the Study of Experimental Medicine*, trans. Henry Copley Green (New York: Dover, 1957), p. 35.

5. Sanvitale, "Postfazione," in Katherine Mansfield, *Lettere e diari: Pagine scelte*, ed. C. K. Stead (Milan: Mondadori, 1981), p. 395.

6. Katherine Mansfield, *The Letters of Katherine Mansfield* (New York: Alfred A. Knopf, 1936), p. 204.

7. Natalia Ginzburg, *É difficile parlare di sé: Conversazione a più voci condotta da Marino Sinibaldi*, ed. Cesare Garboli and Lisa Ginzburg (Torino: Einaudi, 1999), pp. 191–92.

8. Korney Chukovsky, quoted in Vladimir Nabokov, *Lectures on Russian Literature*, ed. Fredson Bowers (New York: Harcourt Brace Jovanovich, 1981), p. 247.

9. Anton Chekhov, "Zapisnye knizhki: knizhka pervaja" ("Notebooks: First Notebook") *Sobranie Sochinenii*, vol. 10 (Moscow: Khudozestvennaia literatura, 1963), p. 482 [L.L. translation]. Chekhov is countering the antimaterialist position articulated in Leo Tolstoy's fable "How Much Land Does a Man Need?"; see Tolstoy, *How Much Land Does a Man Need? and Other Stories*, intr. A. N. Wilson, trans. Ronald Wilkes (London: Penguin, 1994).

10. Lev Shestov, *Anton Tchekhov and Other Essays* (Maunsel & Co., 1916).

11. Constantin Stanislavsky, *My Life in Art* (Theater Arts Books, 1924).

12. Maxim Gorky, *Reminiscences of Anton Chekhov* (B. W. Huebsch, 1921).

13. The characterizations belong, respectively, to the literary historian D. S. Mirsky ("singer of twilight moods," "a poet of superfluous people"), the populist literary critic N. K. Mikhailovsky ("a sick talent," "a poet of anguish"), Yu. Aleksandrovich (pen name of the critic A. N. Poteryakhin) (voice of "world sorrow"), and the theologian Sergei Bulgakov ("optimopessimist"). See also Nina Toumanova, *Anton Chekhov: The Voice of Twilight Russia* (New York: Columbia University Press, 1937). I would eventually discover that Chekhov was just as brutal in his estimate of his fellow Russians. He wrote to his editor Suvorin in 1889, "Russian

writers live in drainpipes, eat slugs, and make love to sluts and laundresses. They know nothing of history, geography, or the natural sciences." Anton Chekhov to Alexei Suvorin, May 15, 1889, in Anton Chekhov, *Perepiska A. P. Chekhova*, available at: *http://www.dushu.com.ua/*. Subsequent citations from Chekhov's correspondence come from this source, and the translations are mine.

14. Anton Chekhov to Alexei Suvorin, September 8, 1891.

15. Anton Chekhov to Alexei Suvorin, May 30, 1888.

16. Ivan Bunin, the Nobel Prize–winning modernist, identified the squalid port on the Sea of Azov as having had a profound influence on Chekhov's "innate melancholy."

"Locals in Taganrog lived in small, dilapidated houses with moth-eaten awnings, tiny gardens, and common latrines. They rendered nothing sacred or private via gossip and news filled with envy and spite. They were also host to cruel spectacles; for example, prisoners were flogged or executed in public squares; stray dogs were beaten to death with clubs and sticks; young girls occasionally were kidnapped for Turkish harems.

"Chekhov never got over his dislike of Taganrog. In fact, the only saving grace about the place was the surrounding sea, its sights, smells, and sounds becoming a hallmark of his writing." (Ivan Bunin, *About Chekhov: The Unfinished Symphony*, ed. and trans. Thomas Gaiton Marullo [Evanston, Ill.: Northwestern University Press, 2007], p. 3)

17. Anton Chekhov to Alexei Suvorin, October 27, 1888.

18. Undated letter (1900), cited in F. Malcovati, "Introduzione," in Anton Cechov, *Racconti* (Milan: Garzanti, 1996), vol. 1, p. xxv.

19. Anton Chekhov to Alexei Suvorin, March 27, 1894.

20. Anton Chekhov to Ivan Ivanovich Orlov, February 22, 1899.

21. Anton Chekhov to Alexei Pleshcheyev, October 4, 1888.

22. Anton Chekhov to Nikolai Chekhov, 1886.

23. A. P. Chudakov and Julian Graffy, "The Poetics of Chekhov: The Sphere of Ideas," *New Literary History*, vol. 9, no. 2, "Soviet Semiotics and Criticism: An Anthology" (Winter 1978): 375.

24. Anton Chekhov, *The Wood-Demon*, act III.

25. Anton Chekhov, "Svirel" ("The Reed Pipe").

26. L. Gol'denveizer, *Vblizi Tolstogo* (Moscow: Gosudarstvennoe izdatel'stvo khudozhestvennoi literatury, 1959), pp. 68–69. Boris Eichenbaum, the Russian formalist critic, notes that Tolstoy recognized Chekhov's radical originality and found in him his only serious competitor. He quotes the novelist as saying, "Chekhov is an incomparable artist, yes, yes: incomparable.... An artist of life ... Chekhov created new forms of writing, completely new, in my opinion, to the entire world, the like of which I have encountered nowhere.... And already it is impossible to compare Chekhov, as an artist, with earlier Russian writers—with Turgenev, with Dostoevsky, or with me. Chekhov has his own special form like the impressionists." Boris Eichenbaum, "Chekhov at Large," *Chekhov: A Collection of Critical Essays*, ed. Robert Louis Jackson (Englewood Cliffs, N.J.: Prentice-Hall, 1967), p. 27.

27. Anton Chekhov to Alexander Chekhov, May 18, 1886.

28. *Dear Writer, Dear Actress: The Love Letters of Anton Chekhov and Olga Knipper*, ed. and trans. Jean Benedetti (Hopewell, N.J.: Ecco Press, 1996).

29. Anton Chekhov to Rimma Vashuk-Neishtadt, March 28, 1897.

30. *Note-Book of Anton Chekhov*, Trans. S. S. Koteliansky and Leonard Woolf, available at: *http://www.gutenberg.org/etext/12494-8.txt*.

# Chapter One

1. Chekhov picks up the metaphors that Gorky uses to describe his literary credentials in a letter from early January 1899: "I am as dumb as a locomotive. Since I was ten I've been on my own. I've had no time for studies; I've done nothing but devour life and work, and meanwhile life's been beating me up and fired my engines and gave me a push—and now, here I am, tearing along at a mad pace. But I've got no rails to run on, and though I see life in a fresh, powerful way, I don't know how to think and so expect I'm headed for disaster.... Maybe my nose won't hit the ground quite yet, but even if it should, I'm not afraid and I'm not sorry." [L.L.]

2. In promoting Chekhov's writings and bringing out collections of his stories, Suvorin, an influential man of letters, was in many ways the force behind Chekhov's popularity. The two met in 1885, became close friends, and even traveled abroad together in 1891 and 1894. Contemporaries marveled at the union of polar opposites represented by the friendship of two men with radically divergent political views. One observer, Dmitry S. Merezhkovsky, quipped, "The devil took up with the infant." [L.L.]

3. Viktor Burenin, the editor of *New Times* (*Novoye Vremya*), gave Chekhov's "The Steppe" a favorable review. A "breakthrough" experimental work, this novella tells the experiences and perceptions of a nine-year-old boy crossing the steppe on his way to boarding school. [L.L.]

4. In October 1888, the Imperial Academy of Sciences awarded Chekhov the prestigious Pushkin Prize for Literature for his collection *In the Twilight*. [L.L.]

5. Chekhov wrote "An Attack of Nerves" ("Pripadok") in 1888 for an anthology commemorating his friend and admirer Vsevolod Garshin, a talented young writer who had committed suicide. Alexei Pleshcheyev, a prominent political exile and civic

poet, was editor of the journal *Northern Herald* (*Severnii Vestnik*), in which Chekhov published a number of stories. Dmitry Grigorovich used his considerable prestige and literary influence to promote Chekhov's stories among key editors and critics. As a venerable elder, he carried on the distinctly Russian tradition of passing on the baton of literary "election" to the worthiest representative of the new writers. His recognition did much to help Chekhov take his own talent seriously. [L.L.]

6. Dmitry Petrovich Golitsyn, a minor talent who wrote under the pseudonym Muravlin, published a number of stories and novels about the aristocracy. [L.L.]

7. Lydia Avilova was a prolific writer and memoirist whose relationship with Chekhov, whom she met in St. Petersburg, remains unclear. Married with children, she had little physical contact with the writer—eight brief encounters in a decade—but made much of them in her reminiscences of their friendship. [L.L.]

8. The talented artist Alexandra Khotyaintseva visited Chekhov's cottage in Melikhovo and charmed him with her sketches and portraits. He invited her to visit him in Nice, where she took up residence in his Russian hotel and amused him with caricatures of its residents. [L.L.]

9. Chekhov lived, worked, and entertained in Melikhovo, south of Moscow, between 1860 and 1904. In 1892, after his return from Sakhalin, he bought an estate, where his entire family settled, and wrote some of his most memorable works, including his plays, in this delightful rural retreat. Generous with his time, energy, and funds, he constructed model schools in three villages, served as a member of the local administrative organization, the *zemstvo*, and in all ways became an exemplar of civic consciousness. This public role did not prevent him, however, from acting the generous host to countless friends, associates, admirers, and hangers-on. [L.L.]

10. The "thick journals" (*tolstye zhurnaly*), two-hundred-plus-page periodicals, were the cultural lifeline of imperial Russia. Compendia of fiction, nonfiction, poetry, criticism, and articles on everything from philosophy to agronomy, these monthlies, which were distributed by subscription and by book dealers, furnished topics for endless debate. Among the most influential nineteenth-century thick journals were *Herald of Europe* (*Vestnik Evropy*), *Library for Reading* (*Biblioteka Dlya Chteniya*), *Notes of the Fatherland* (*Otechestvennye Zapiski*), *The Contemporary* (*Sovremennik*), *Russian Messenger* (*Russkiy Vestnik*), and *Russian Thought* (*Russkaya Mysl'*). [L.L.]

11. "Perepiska A. P. Chekhova" ("Pis'ma Chekhova"), no. 2850, p. 137, available at: http://www.dushu.com.ua/.

12. The *Northern Herald* (*Severniy Vestnik*) was a liberal thick journal published in St. Petersburg from 1885 to 1898. [L.L.]

13. The St. Petersburg *New Times* (*Novoye Vremya*), the largest newspaper in Russia, was owned by Alexei Suvorin, who was also its editor in chief. Pro-government, right-wing, and not infrequently anti-Semitic and reactionary, the paper nevertheless embraced an enlightened cultural policy and did much to nurture the talents of young writers. [L.L.]

14. Ignaty Nikolaevich Potapenko (1826–1929) was an overrated writer of fiction and plays, including *The General's Daughter* (1892), to which Chekhov here alludes. [L.L.]

15. Maria Kiselyova was one of the many cultivated, accomplished women whom Chekhov, a man not indifferent to female intelligence and beauty, playfully courted during his protracted bachelorhood. An accomplished writer, Kiselyova often turned to Chekhov for advice. [L.L.]

16. In "The Black Monk" ("Chornyj monakh") (1894), Chekhov offers a luminous exploration of a Romantic cliché—the psychopathological creative genius. Informed by contemporary

medical science, the story is prescient in its exploration of sociological and ecological issues. [L.L.]

17. Chekhov's youngest brother, Mikhail Pavlovich. [L.L.]

18. Alexei Suvorin's first wife, Anna Ivanovna Suvorina (neé Baranova, 1840–74) was a talented writer and a translator of, among others, Jules Verne. His second wife was also Anna Ivanovna (1858–1936). [L.L.]

19. *Eugene Onegin* (*Evgeniy Onegin*, 1833), A. S. Pushkin's novel in verse, and Leo Tolstoy's *Anna Karenina* (1877) became instant classics and set the bar for aesthetic virtuosity when they appeared. [L.L.]

20. The provisional title of this novel was "Stories from the Lives of My Friends." After two years of work, Chekhov decided to destroy the manuscript, fearing that it would never get by the censor. [L.L.]

21. Elena Shavrova, a friend of Chekhov's sister Maria, developed a fierce crush on the writer as an adolescent. For many years Chekhov appointed himself her reader, critic, tutor, editor, and "agent." In his letters, he addressed her as "Most esteemed colleague" and signed himself "Cher maitre." [L.L.]

22. Syphilis is the topic in question. [L.L.]

23. The Pushkin Prize; see n. 4. [L.L.]

24. With its subtle echoes of Tolstoy's *Anna Karenina* and muted satirical sketches, "The Name Day Party" ("Imeniny," 1888) was one of Chekhov's most brilliant "clinical" stories of the late 1880s and early 1890s. [L.L.]

25. Lazarev-Gruzinsky's reminiscences recall Chekhov's help with publishing his stories, his love of mushrooming, and his wicked sense of humor. [L.L.]

26. Anna Mikhailovna Evreinova (1844–?) would become editor of the St. Petersburg journal *Northern Herald* in 1889–90. [L.L.]

27. Ieronim Ieronimovich Yasinsky (1850–1930) was a minor writer of shifting loyalties and wildly fluctuating political affiliations who wrote under the pseudonyms M. Chunosov and Maksim Belinsky. Dmitry Narkisovich Mamin (1852–1912) wrote novels about life in the Urals under the pseudonym Mamin-Sibiryak. Nikolay Fedotovich Bazhin (1843–1908) was a mildly successful, derivative novelist and chronicler of contemporary life in the manner of "sober realism." [L.L.]

## Chapter Two

1. Isaac Ilych Levitan (1860–1900), one of Russia's finest landscape painters, was a close friend of Chekhov's and shared the writer's nuanced eye for color, atmosphere, and understatement. [L.L.]

2. Prince Andrei, Natasha, and Sonya are characters in Leo Tolstoy's novel *War and Peace*, set in the time of the Napoleonic Wars. [L.L.]

3. As cited in F. Malcovati, "Introduzione" in Anton Cechov, *Racconti* (Milan: Garzanti, 1996), vol. 1, p. xxv.

4. Denis Vasilevich Davydov (1784–1839), a gifted lyrical poet, member of the Pushkin Pleiade, and hero of the War of 1812, is known especially for his verses in praise of wine, women, and song. [L.L.]

5. See "General Questions," n. 5.

6. Writer Osip Konstantinovich Notovich (1849–1914), a fellow alumnus of the Taganrog Boys' Gymnasium, was briefly the publisher of *New Times* (*Novoye Vremya*) and the author of plays and quasi-philosophical tracts for the mass market. The journalist Grigory Konstantinovich Gradovsky (1842–1915) wrote popular feuilletons under the pseudonym Gamma and a number of weak plays. Neither was distinguished by high principles. [L.L.]

7. Alexander Zhirkevich, though a discriminating consumer of cultural artifacts, was a plodding writer who nonetheless managed to publish a respectable number of stories. Chekhov never turned down a request for advice; consequently, his writing desk was always piled high with the manuscripts of aspiring writers. [L.L.]

8. This is indeed one of Gorky's strongest and most anthologized stories about desperate men in desperate places. [L.L.]

9. Chekhov is referring to characters in the "problem" novels of Ivan Turgenev (1818–83): Lavretsky and Liza from *A Nest of Gentlefolk* (1859); Elena from *On the Eve* (1860); Bazarov, Odintsova, and Kukshina from *Fathers and Sons* (1862); and Irina from *Smoke* (1867). Leo Tolstoy's *Anna Karenina* appeared in installments in the *Russian Messenger* between 1873 and 1877. [L.L.]

10. A *zemstvo*, or elective district council, was a local administrative unit established in 1864 as part of the reforms associated with the emancipation of the serfs in 1861; it remained in place until 1917. Membership was restricted to members of the nobility and the bourgeoisie. [L.L.]

11. "Sakhalin Fugitive" ("Sokolinets") is one of a cycle of stories in which the author, Vladimir Korolenko, drew on his own experiences of exile in Siberia. Published in 1885, the piece played a seminal role in Chekhov's evolution, inspiring the musical construction of "Steppe" and providing an impetus for undertaking his own Sakhalin project. [L.L.]

12. Syphilis. [L.L.]

13. Dmitry Sergeyevich Merezhkovsky (1866–1941), poet, novelist, critic, philosopher, and translator, was one of the key figures of the Russian Silver Age of modernism. He was only twenty-two when he reviewed Chekhov's story "On Easter Eve" ("Svyatoyu Noch'yu") (1886), in which the monk Ieronim appears. [L.L.]

14. Suvorin's servant. [L.L.]

15. Kulakov is the pen name of a minor contributor to Leykin's humorous magazine *Fragments* (*Oskol'ki*). [L.L.]

16. "Fires" ("Ogni") (1888) is a story that touches on the predicament of women in a society that limits their options for self-determination. It closes with the line "You can't make sense of anything in this world." [L.L.]

17. Chekhov is punning on his correspondent's surname, which is derived from the Russian word *shchegol,* meaning "goldfinch." [L.L.]

18. The Fontanka is a small river in St. Petersburg. [L.L.]

19. Vukol Lavrov was the owner, publisher, and editor of the Moscow left-liberal literary journal *Russian Thought (Russkaya Mysl').* [L.L.]

20. Chekhov is responding to Lavrov's swipe at him in *Russian Thought*: "Only yesterday the high priests of unprincipled writing, like Messrs. Yasinsky and Chekhov...." For the preceding four years, Chekhov had been subjected to a barrage of criticism for his "indifference," "lack of engagement," and "absence of principles." He finally decided to put a stop to this chronic objection to his work—stemming from a particularly Russian insistence that writers solve the problems of the world—on the eve of his departure for Sakhalin. [L.L.]

21. Grigory Aleksandrovich Machtet (1852–1901), who began his literary career in San Francisco and published a number of sketches about life in the United States, was a contributor to *Russian Thought.* [L.L.]

22. This letter of resignation was quoted in a letter to Vladimir Korolenko, Yalta, August 25, 1902. [L.L.]

23. In 1900 Chekhov, along with Tolstoy and Korolenko, was among the ten writers selected by the Academy of Sciences for full membership in the newly formed Pushkin Section of Belles Lettres. In December 1901, he learned that A. M. Peshkov, who wrote under the pen name Maxim Gorky, had been elected to the Academy. Two weeks later, the honor was withdrawn in light of Gorky's prison record for illegal political activities. Pressed by

friends and Korolenko, Chekhov resigned his own membership in protest. [L.L.]

24. The surgeon Ivan Orlov was an exceptionally idealistic and effective organizer of rural medicine, especially in the environs of Moscow. His exemplary clinic was recognized as a mecca by rural physicians. Orlov treated a number of prominent Russian writers and intellectuals, among them the Symbolist poet Alexander Blok, and was a close friend and associate of Chekhov, with whom he corresponded intensely from 1889 to 1899. Chekhov's entire letter is written in a solemn, ecclesiastical style, prompted by Orlov's letter, which draws on a scriptural passage to condemn local authorities for their mishandling of medical service in rural areas. [L.L.]

25. As cited in Malcovati, "Introduzione" vol. 1, p. xxv.

26. Chekhov and Suvorin had a serious disagreement leading to a rupture that lasted several months over the notorious case of Captain Alfred Dreyfus, the French army officer who had been court-martialed and condemned to life imprisonment in 1894 for allegedly spying in the interests of Germany. Chekhov followed the case avidly and was especially moved by the open letter of Émile Zola, "J'accuse," in which the French novelist charged the government and the War Office with suppressing key evidence that demonstrated Dreyfus's innocence. Suvorin had written a column in *New Times* accusing Zola of publicity mongering. [L.L.]

27. S. I. Erber and Mikhail Mikhailovich Chemodanov contributed drawings and caricatures to the St. Petersburg journal *Oskol'ki* (*Fragments*). Chemodanov (1856–1908), like Chekhov, was a physician with a second career.

28. The reference is to a wave of student unrest that swept Russian universities in February and March 1899. The unrest began in response to a university anniversary celebration in St. Petersburg that was brutally put down by mounted police. Sympathy strikes were called in other universities. A blackout on press coverage of the disturbances was imposed early in March, and by

the middle of that month both Moscow and St. Petersburg universities were temporarily closed. Suvorin's paper, *New Times*, took an anti-strike position. [L.L.]

## Chapter Three

1. Friedrich Alexander von Humboldt (1769–1859), German scientist and traveler, explored the far eastern reaches of the Russian Empire in 1829 at the request of the czarist government, while the American journalist George Kennan (1845–1924) visited Siberian prisons in 1886 and wrote about them in *Siberia and the Exile System* (1891). [L.L.]

2. The twelve-month siege of Sebastopol in 1854–55, which was key in Russia's defeat in the Crimean War against the allied forces of the British, French, and Piedmontese, resulted in tremendous casualties on both sides. [L.L.]

3. The 1860s were the decade of major reforms, among them the emancipation of the serfs, who made up approximately 80 percent of the population of Russia. [L.L.]

4. "Sakhalin mania" (Latin). [L.L.]

5. Marina Konstantinovna Tsebrikova (1835–1917) was a prominent writer, journalist, and activist for women's education and rights who began her literary activity as a member of the politically engaged generation of the 1860s. [L.L.]

6. Chekhov uses the archaic name for Russia to evoke the famous observation, made in the eleventh century *Primary Chronicle*, that there was no order among the indigenous East Slavic tribes of Rus'. [L.L.]

7. A. I. Voyeykov (1842–1916) was an outstanding, pioneering meteorologist, climatologist, and geographer who introduced the scientific study of weather by means of monitoring stations. An indefatigable traveler, he produced a series of climatological maps

and, among many works, the monumental *Climates of Various Lands/Climates of the Earth, with Special Reference to Russia* (*Klimaty raznyx stran/Klimaty zemnogo shara, v osobennosti Rossii*) published in 1884 and in an expanded edition in 1887. [L.L.]

8. Sergey V. Maksimov (1831–1901), ethnographer, writer, and member of the St. Petersburg Academy of Sciences, was the author of literary ethnographic sketches, voluminous studies on the ethnography of the Russian Far East, and the three-volume *Siberia and Penal Servitude* (*Sibir' i katorga*) (St. Petersburg, 1871). [L.L.]

9. Chekhov added the following footnote: "One should note here an observation made by Nevelskoy that the indigenous people usually draw a line between shores in order to indicate that it is possible to sail from shore to shore: that is, to point out the existence of a strait between the shorelines." [L.L.]

10. Jean Baptiste Bourguignon d'Anville (1697–1782), author of the *Nouvel atlas de la Chine, de la Tartaire chinoise, et de Thibet* (1737). [A.C.]

## Chapter Four

1. This archetypically Russian footwear is known as a *valenok* (plural: *valenki*). Made of wool felt and resembling rubber galoshes, valenki are best worn in dry weather. [L.L.]

2. The Roman numerals in brackets refer to chapters in *The Island of Sakhalin*. [L.L.]

3. *Shtoss* is a game of chance played with cards, with rules similar, though not identical, to faro, which features prominently in Russian fiction of the Romantic period in such famous stories as A. S. Pushkin's "Queen of Spades" and Mikhail Lermontov's "Shtoss." [L.L.]

4. Chekhov gives an approximate translation of Cassio's lines in act 2, scene 1, of William Shakespeare's *Othello*. [L.L.]

5. Chekhov elsewhere explains that this was the name for three pointed reefs lying beyond the mouth of the Duyka River. [L.L.]

6. The Nativity of the Virgin Mary is celebrated on September 8 according to the Russian Orthodox calendar. [L.L.]

7. The shopkeeper, subsequently called "L" in the text, was the nobleman K. Kh. Landsberg, a Guards officer accused of a savage murder and sentenced to penal servitude in 1879. [L.L.]

8. In a letter to Suvorin dated December 2, 1896, Chekhov identifies this postmaster as Eduard Duchinsky, author of poetry and prose. *Sakhalinó* was intended to parody *Borodinó* (1837), a patriotic poem about the 1812 battle of Borodinó—the last fought by Napoleon on Russian soil—by the Romantic poet and writer Mikhail Lermontov. [L.L.]

9. A verst is equivalent to 3,500 feet, or 1.0668 kilometers. [L.L.]

10. Fertile black soil. [L.L.]

11. It took us three hours to cover the four miles from Uskovo to Voskresenskoye. If readers can imagine a man on foot loaded down with flour, salted beef, and assorted government supplies, or a sick person from Uskovo having to go to the Rykov hospital, they will understand what the phrase "There is no road" means on Sakhalin. It is impossible to travel by carriage or on horseback. It has happened that attempts to go on horseback have ended with horses breaking their legs. [A.C.]

12. Sakhalin fever (Latin). [L.L.]

13. The offering of bread and salt is a traditional gesture of welcome to guests in Russian households. [L.L.]

14. He also raised very unrealistic hopes. In one village, speaking of the fact that peasant exiles now had the right to return to the mainland, he said, "And later you can also return to your homeland, to Russia." [A.C.]

15. The best description of this quintessentially Russian conveyance can be found in Count K. K. Pahlen's 1908–1909 memoir

*Mission to Turkestan*: "Has the reader any idea what the vehicle called tarantass in Russian is really like? Capable of being driven over rocks, boulders or, as a matter of fact, over any imaginable surface, it must have been invented in the days when no roads existed at all. It consists of two long, springy poles, about four inches thick, placed parallel and bridging the two wheel axles to which they are attached. A large wickerwork body, broad enough to hold two people, is placed between the two poles in the center between the axles. A light seat is sometimes fixed inside the body, and the more luxurious tarantasses are provided with a hood. The coachman perches on a small seat over the fore-axle and the whole contraption is harnessed to three horses, the one in the center running between two shafts. When passengers are about to leave a posting inn, a mattress covered with a feather blanket is spread over the bottom of the body. With a little luck one is able to snatch some sleep stretched out at full length provided the going is not too rough. In theory, the springy poles are supposed to take up the bumping, but in actual practice they are usually so stiff and strong for the sake of solidity that one is mercilessly jolted about or bounced to and fro if the pace is hot. Because of this, and the fact that as an inspecting Senator and consequently an important personage I was always driven at top speed, we called the tarantass a 'horse-powered liver-massaging device.'" K. K. Pahlen, "Selections from *Mission to Turkestan: Being the Memoirs of Count K. K. Pahlen, 1908–1909*," trans. N. Couriss, available at: www.iras.ucalgary.ca/ ~volk/sylvia/Pahlen.htm (last updated August 14, 2001; accessed January 20, 2007). [L.L.]

16. In his personification of the waves, Chekhov echoes the Russian Romantic poet F. I. Tyutchev, specifically the 1848 poem "The Sea and the Cliff." [L.L.]

17. Known as *nary*, these sleeping platforms were low wooden benches arranged down the center of the room and taking up

about half of its width. Along the longitudinal axis, the benches sloped slightly toward the center, so that the prisoners slept head to head in the middle, with their feet, a few inches lower, at the outer edges of the benches. [L.L.]

18. These figures, taken from church baptismal records, represent only the Orthodox population. [A.C.]

19. In 1722 Emperor Peter I, the Great, rationalized and standardized government service by instituting a "Table of Ranks," comprising fourteen "grades" in the military, the civil, and the court services, respectively, with prescribed duties, obligations, benefits, privileges, rights, and prerogatives, as well as distinctive uniforms, assigned to each. A collegiate registrar served in the bureaucracy's lowest, or fourteenth, rank. [L.L.]

20. To date, the two individuals who have done the most for the establishment and responsible management of the penal colony are M. S. Mitsul and M. N. Galkin-Vraskoy. A tiny, impoverished, temporary settlement of ten households is named in honor of the former, while a settlement with the long-established local name Silyantsy was named for the latter, though it is known as Galinko-Vraskoye only on some maps. Incidentally, the name of M. S. Korsakov was given to a settlement and a large post not because of any of his particular merits or sacrifices, but simply because he had once served as Governor General and had made himself feared. [A.C.]

21. Cabbage soup. [L.L.]

22. Anton Chekhov, "Iz Sibiri," II (May 9, 1890), *Polnoe sobranie sochinenii i pisem v tridcati tomakh: Sochinenia v vosemnadcati tomakh: Toma chetyrnadcatyj—pyatnadcatyj: Iz Sibiri: Ostrov Sakhalin. (1890–1995)* (Moscow: Nauka, 1987), available at: http://az.lib.ru/c/chehow_a_p/text_0200.shtml.

23. On the consecration of the Krilon lighthouse by Bishop Martimian, see *Vladivostok*, 1883, no. 28. [A.C.]

24. Chekhov is giving the temperature in Réamur units, which were standard in Russia in the eighteenth and nineteenth centuries. The equivalent temperature in Fahrenheit is 32 degrees. [L.L.]

25. Personal proper names, in Russia, reflect the patriarchal structure of the society. Every individual is known by his or her given name (corresponding to our first name), followed by the patronymic—the given name of the father to which the suffix "-ovich" (masculine) or "-ovna" (feminine) is added—and finally, the surname (family name). Personal address is extremely complex in Russia. Subtle nuances of status, degree of intimacy, and esteem can be communicated, depending on which part or parts of the triadic name are used, and in what combination; whether or not diminutive forms of any parts of these names are used; and finally, if a diminutive is used, which of nearly a dozen variants of diminutives the speaker chooses to use. [L.L.]

26. The Old Believers, or "Raskol'niki," were a conservative Russian Orthodox sect formed in the midseventeenth century in opposition to reforms in church ritual and books introduced and enforced by Patriarch Nikon on the contemporary Greek Orthodox model. Subject to excommunication and persecution, the Old Believers retreated to the easternmost territories of the Russian Empire and, after the Revolution of 1917, found their way to refuges in China, Argentina, Canada, and the United States, where they have remained to this day. [L.L.]

27. Potemkin was already a rich man when he arrived on Sakhalin. Dr. Avgustinovich, who saw him three years after his arrival on Sakhalin, wrote, "The home of the exile Potemkin is the best." If in only three years Potemkin, as a convict, was able to build himself a good house, keep horses, and marry his daughter off to a Sakhalin official, then, I think, agriculture had nothing to do with his success. [A.C.]

28. The melodrama *Trente ans, ou La vie d'un jouer* (1827) was written by French novelist and playwright Victor Henri-Joseph Brahain du Cange (or Ducange) (1783–1833). [L.L.]

29. Situated some 1,800 miles east of Tomsk, in the Siberian Transbaikal, were the mines of Kara, where the czarist regime banished the most dangerous criminals and the most troublesome political offenders. [L.L.]

30. Chekhov's footnote bearing on this settler's verbal virtuosity is cited earlier in the *Notebook* section. [L.L.]

## Chapter Five

1. Sintsovsky, "Hygienic Conditions of Convicts, Correspondence (from Western Siberia) from the Island of Sakhalin," *Zdorov'e*, no. 16 (1875). [A.C.]

2. For more detail, see A. M. Nikol'sky, *Sakhalin Island and Its Vertebrate Fauna* (*Ostrov Sakhalin I ego fauma pozvonochnykh zhivotnykh*), supp. to vol. 9, *Zapiski im. Akademii Nauk* (St. Petersburg, 1889). [A.C.]

3. The agronomist Mikhail Semyonovich Mitsul'—a man of rare moral strength, an indefatigable worker, optimist, and idealist, endowed with enthusiasm and the capacity of communicating it to others—also took part in the expedition under the command of Vlasov that was dispatched from St. Petersburg in 1870. At that time Mitsul' was in his midthirties. He was exceptionally conscientious in discharging the duties with which he had been entrusted. In studying the soil, flora, and fauna of Sakhalin, he covered on foot the entire area encompassed by the present Aleksandrovsk and Tymovsk regions, the western coast, and the entire southern part of the island. At that time, there were no roads on the island; the miserable paths that did exist here and there disappeared in the taiga and in the swamps, and any form of

transportation, by horse or on foot, was a veritable martyrdom. The idea of a convict agricultural colony both astonished and fascinated Mitsul'. He embraced it with his entire soul and came to love Sakhalin. Like a mother, for whom her beloved child can do no wrong, Mitsul' paid no attention to the frozen earth and the fogs of the island that had become his second motherland. Instead, he saw it as a flourishing garden, and from this opinion he could be moved neither by the meteorological record, which, in all fairness, was nearly nonexistent at the time, nor by the bitter experiences of earlier visitors, of whose value he was profoundly skeptical. Here, after all, could be found wild grapes, bamboo, gigantic grasses.... The subsequent history of the island finds him in the role of Actual State Councilor, as enthusiastic and indefatigable as ever. He died on Sakhalin of an acute nervous ailment at the age of forty-one. I saw his grave. He left behind a book, *An Agricultural Study of Sakhalin* (1873). It is an extensive paean to the fertility of Sakhalin. [A.C.]

4. In the interest of fairness, I should note that Mayor Sh. showed perfect respect for my literary profession and that for the duration of my stay in Korsakov, he made every effort to rescue me from boredom. Several weeks before my arrival in the south, he had made the same exertions on behalf of the Englishman Howard, an adventurer and a man of letters, who had survived shipwreck on a Japanese [*sic*] junk on the Aniva and subsequently wrote some rubbish about the Ainus in his book *The Life with Trans-Siberian Savages*. [A.C.]

5. Volunteer. [L.L.]

6. According to the "Regulations on Exiles," authorities are not bound by the procedural directives stipulated in the "Laws of Legal Procedures" when arresting a deported convict. The latter can be arrested at any time under the mere suspicion of having committed a crime. [A.C.]

7. Chekhov is referring to the character of Margarete/Gretchen, the lovely innocent who was seduced and abandoned in Johann Wolfgang Von Goethe's *Faust* (1806–32). [L.L.]

8. The wheelbarrow shackle was a particularly severe form of punishment in which the prisoner was chained to a wooden wheelbarrow weighing as much as 175 pounds. Nothing was transported in the wheelbarrow, and the convict thus secured did not engage in any labor. This form of punishment was reserved for escapees, recidivists, and those sentenced to death penalty but pardoned. [L.L.]

9. [Tolstykh] was sentenced to penal servitude for beheading his wife. [A.C.]

10. The Russian peasant hut featured a large, high, usually tiled stove, the top of which was used as a sleeping platform. [L.L.]

11. In other words, he occupied the highest rank in the lowest of the fourteen grades in the "Table of Ranks." See ch. 4, n. 19. [L.L.]

12. Named for Metropolitan Macarius (Mikhail Petrovich Bulgakov, 1816–82), Metropolitan of Moscow and Kolomna and member of many learned societies, including the Russian Academy of Sciences, the Metropolitan Macarius Award was given for exceptional contributions to science. [L.L.]

13. Yakov Alekseevich Korneyev was Chekhov's landlord in Moscow.

## Afterword

1. Anton Chekhov to Grigory Rossolimo, October 11, 1899, in Anton Chekhov, *Epistolario*, ed. Gigliola Venturi and Clara Croïsson, vol. 1 (Turin: Einaudi, 1960).

2. Raymond Carver, "Errand," in *Where I'm Calling From: Selected Stories* (New York: Vintage Books, 1988), pp. 512–13.

3. "I am dying" (German). [L.L.]

4. Olga's account is taken from *Dear Writer . . . Dear Actress: The Love Letters of Olga Knipper and Anton Chekhov*, sel., trans., and ed. Jean Benedetti (London: Methuen Drama, 1998), p. 284.

5. Anton Chekhov to K. S. Filippov, February 2, 1890, in Anton Chekhov, *A Journey to Sakhalin* (Cambridge: Ian Faulkner Publishing, 1993), p. 366. [L.L.]

6. Anton Chekhov to Ivan Leontyev (Shcheglov), March 22, 1890.

7. Anton Chekhov to Alexei Suvorin, March 9, 1890.

8. Anton Chekhov to Alexei Suvorin, February 17, 1890, in Chekhov, *A Journey to Sakhalin*, p. 368. [P.B.]

9. Anton Chekhov, "Nikolai Mikhailovich Przhevalsky," published anonymously in *New Times*, October 26, 1888, and attributed to Chekhov based on a letter from him to E. Lintvaryova, October 27, 1888, in Anton Chekhov, *Opere varie* (Milan: Mursia, 1963), pp. 467–69. Readers both within and outside Russia closely followed the Russian explorer's exploits. Peter Kropotkin wrote about him for the *New Times* drawing on reports published in the *Bulletin of the Russian Geographical Society*; see Kropotkin, *Memorie di un rivoluzionario* (Milan: Feltrinelli, 1969), p. 281. [P.B.]

10. Anton Chekhov to Natalya Lintvaryova, March 5, 1890, in Anton Chekhov, *A Journey to Sakhalin*, p. 370. For representative views on Sakhalin among Russian officials and functionaries, see Howard B. Douglas, *Life with Trans-Siberian Savages* (London: Longmans, 1893), pp. 1–19. [P.B.]

11. Anton Chekhov to Alexei Suvorin, Moscow, March 9, 1890.

12. Anton Chekhov to Alexei Suvorin, Moscow, February 23, 1890.

13. Anton Chekhov to Alexei Pleshcheyev, February 15, 1890.

14. Chekhov's request came at a sensitive time. In an effort to stem negative reports on the czarist penal system by Russian polit-

ical exiles in the West, Galkin-Vraskoy was just then organizing the Fourth International Congress on Penal Servitude in St. Petersburg. He was also overseeing the publication of an official review of the czarist penal system that sought to counter negative reports.

15. At Sakhalin, political prisoners made up about 40 percent of the roughly ten thousand exiles, but their treatment was the principal cause for the czarist government's coming under attack, particularly at that time. "The year 1889 would remain ineradicably imprinted in the memories of those who were at that time prisoners in Siberia," the revolutionary Leo Deutsch wrote in his memoirs. That year, after a long hunger strike among female prisoners at Kara, one female prisoner died after being flogged, and other women committed suicide by poisoning themselves. In Yakutsk, guards bayoneted and shot male and female students who had protested forced marches over long distances on foot without halts; three prisoners were hung, and nineteen were sentenced to hard labor for life. Leo G. Deutsch, *Sedici anni in Siberia: Memorie di un rivoluzionario russo* (Milan: Sonzogno, 1905), pp. 247–63, quotation from p. 250.

16. This summary of Chekhov's journey is based on a selection of letters published in Italian in Anton Chekhov, *Epistolario*, ed. Gigliola Venturi and Clara Croïsson, vol. 1 (Turin: Einaudi, 1960), from which the citations are taken, and on the fuller selection found in *Letters of Anton Chekhov to His Family and Friends: With Biographical Sketch*, ed. Constance Garnett (New York: Macmillan, 1920), now available at: http://www.gutenberg .net/etext/6408. Additionally, use was made of introductory materials from various editions of *The Island of Sakhalin*, in particular by Robert Payne in Anton Chekhov, *The Island: A Journey to Sakhalin*, trans. Luba and Michael Terpak (New York: Washington Square, 1967); Irina Ratushinskaya (London: Folio Society, 1989); Brian Reeve, *A Journey to Sakhalin* (Cambridge: Ian

Faulkner Publishing, 1993); Sophie Lazarus (Grenoble: Éditions Cent Pages, 1995); Roger Grenier (Paris: Gallimard, 2001); and Juras T. Ryfa, "The History of the Journey," in *The Problem of Genre* (Lewiston, Maine: Edwin Mellen, 1999), pp. 26–54. For descriptions of travels in Siberia and on the tarantass, see Luchino Dal Verme, *Giappone e Siberia: Note di viaggio* (Milan, 1882), pp. 402–3,411–12.

17. Anton Chekhov to Alexei Suvorin, Steamship *Baikal*, Strait of Tartary, September 11, 1890.

18. Anton Chekhov to Alexei Suvorin, August 16, 1892.

19. Anton Chekhov to Alexei Suvorin, Melikhovo, July 28, 1893.

20. Brian Reeve, "Introduction," pp. 27–28; Ryfa, *The Problem of Genre*, pp. 91–96, 152–53.

21. Anton Chekhov, *Zapisnye knizhki* (Moscow: Gosudarstvennoe izdatel'stvo khudozhestvennoj literatury, 1950), p. 206.

22. Anton Chekhov to Dmitry Grigorovich, Moscow, February 5, 1888.

23. Anton Chekhov to Alexei Suvorin, Moscow, April 24, 1899.

24. Anton Chekhov to Maria Kiselyova, Moscow, January 14, 1887.

25. Vladimir Nabokov, *Lectures on Russian Literature*, ed. and intro. Fredson Bowers (New York: Harcourt, 1981), p. 246.

26. Anton Chekhov to Alexei Suvorin, Melikhovo, August 1, 1892.

27. Anton Chekhov to Alexei Suvorin, Nice, February 6, 1898.

28. Anton Chekhov to Ivan Orlov, Yalta, February 22, 1899.

29. Anton Chekhov to Alexander Chekhov, Moscow, September 7, 1887.

30. Anton Chekhov to Alexei Pleshcheyev, Moscow, October 4, 1888.